Contents

KU-379-856

Introduction

1. The Framework of Law

Emerald Law

The English Legal System

Anthony Chadwick

B037986

Emerald Publishing
www.emeraldpublishing.co.uk

British Cataloguing in Publication data. A catalogue record is available for this book from the British Library.

ISBN 978-1-84716-378-3

Grosvenor Group (Print Services) Ltd, London

Cover Design by Bookworks Islington

Whilst every effort has been made to ensure that the information in this book is accurate at the time of going to print, the author and publisher recognise that the information can become out of date. The book is therefore sold on the understanding that no responsibility for errors and omissions is assumed and no responsibility is held for the information held within.

Introduction

This second edition of Emerald Law-Guide to the English Legal System is wide ranging and covers all the main areas of our complex legal system in depth.

The English Legal System is the domestic legal system of England and Wales, including courts and tribunals, procedure, legal aid and also the people operating the system, i.e. judges, magistrates, solicitors and barristers, jurors and tribunal members.

For the average person, the legal system in this country can appear mystifying. All they know is that the process of funding legal cases costs a lot of money. However, for most of us in our lives, one way or another, we will find ourselves in court. The need for good advice will be paramount.

It is very important for a citizen to have a clear idea of how the legal system operates and who is who in the system, the role of the judiciary, the European Courts and also the availability of funding if a case needs to go to court and is proving to expensive.

One of the main axioms of the last ten years or so has been access to justice. How easily can individuals and others access the legal system in this country. With the advent of the coalition government it seems that legal aid will be restricted making it harder for people to access legal advice.

This introduction to the English legal System should prove invaluable to all, student, professional and layperson.

Anthony Chadwick

1

The Framework of Law

Law covers a wide variety of areas. There are different categories of law: national law; international law which is divided into public and private law and further sub-categories discussed later.

International law

International law concerns itself with inter-nation disputes and conflict. This law, in the main, derives from various treaties which have been agreed over time betwee
n different governments.

National law

This is the law which applies within each individual nation. Within national law there is a distinction between public and private law. Public law involves the government or state in some way and private law is concerned with disputes and conflict between individuals and businesses. Public and private law, as mentioned can be further sub-divided.

Public law

There are three distinct areas of public law:

1. Constitutional law

Constitutional law controls and sets out the framework for government, and methods of government.

2. Administrative law

This controls how the ministers of government, both national and local, can operate. A key part of administrative law is that of the right to judicial review of decisions made by government.

3. Criminal law

Criminal law deals with the types of behaviour, whether individual or on a business level, which are considered outside the boundaries of the general law and accepted moral codes and which are punishable. A person who commits a crime is said to have offended against the State and the State has the right to prosecute them and punish them if found guilty.

Private law

Private law is usually termed civil law and there are many differing branches. The main ones dealing with everyday matters are family law, contract law, tort (negligence), company law and employment law. Civil law is very different in nature from criminal law. Whereas criminal law deals with crimes against the state, private or civil law deals with disputes between individuals

Distinctions between criminal law cases and civil cases

There are key differences between criminal and civil cases. The cases take place in different courts. In general, criminal law cases will be heard in either Magistrates Courts or the Crown Court. Civil cases are heard either in the High Court or, more often than not, in the County Court. Some civil cases, especially matters concerning family, can be heard in the Magistrates Court.

In criminal cases, the terminology used to describe key personnel is different to that of those involved in civil cases. The person commencing a criminal case is called a prosecutor, whilst in civil cases they are called the claimant.

In criminal cases, the terminology used generally is different. A person is either found guilty or not guilty. In a civil case a defendant is found liable or not liable. At the end of a criminal case, the person, if found guilty, will be punished and sentenced appropriately. In a civil case, the person if found to be liable will be ordered to put right the matter. This is usually done by an award of money as compensation, known as damages although other remedies may be ordered.

In criminal cases, the standard of proof is very high. A criminal case must be proven beyond all reasonable doubt. Civil cases are proved on the balance of probabilities. This is a lower standard of proof.

Overleaf is a summary of civil and criminal law cases.

	Civil cases	Criminal cases
Object of law	To uphold the rights of individuals	To maintain law and order
Person starting case	Individuals who are affected	Usually State through police or Crown Prosecution Service
Terminology	Claimant	Prosecutor
Courts	County Court or High Court or Tribunal	Magistrates court or Crown Court
Standard of proof	The balance of probability	Beyond reasonable doubt
People making Decision	Judge	Magistrates or jury
Decision	Liable or not liable	Guilty or not guilty
Powers of court	Usually damages, injunction, performance of contract rescission or rectification	Prison, fine, community order, discharge etc.

Defining law

Having considered the various divisions of law it is now time to consider definitions of law. One broad definition of law was that provided by Sir John Salmond. He defined the law as being 'the body of principles recognised and applied by the state in the administration of justice'. This neatly encapsulates the meaning and application of law in one brief sentence.

Law applies throughout a country to people generally. There are other sets of rules applied more individually to people and organisations, for example rules governing sports or rules which have developed as a result of local customs and traditions.

Law and morality

Moral values of communities set out a framework for how people should behave. Concepts of morality differ from culture to culture, although there are common denominators, for example outlawing extreme and harmful behaviour such as rape or murder. Morality often springs from a religious base, the bible for Christians and the Koran for Muslims are key examples. The law of a country will, usually, reflect the moral values accepted by most of a country but will differ in certain aspects. One example is that adultery is often considered a crime in Muslim countries but not so in Christian countries.

In England and Wales there has been a move away from religious belief and the development of law reflects this. For example a limited form of euthanasia has been accepted as legal, as reflected in the ruling in Airedale NHS Trust v Bland (1993), where it was ruled that medical staff could withdraw life support systems from a patient who could breathe unaided but who was in a persistent vegetative state.

A similar question arose in the case of Diane Pretty in 2001, a 43-year-old woman, suffering Motor Neurone Disease. Diane Pretty's legal action concerned the question of assisted suicide. As the law stands, it is an offence to assist another person to commit suicide under section 2(1) of the Suicide Act 1961. Mrs Pretty asked the Director of Public Prosecution (DPP) to give an undertaking not to prosecute her husband, should he assist her to commit suicide in accordance with her wishes.

The DPP refused permission which was upheld by the High Court in August 2001 and the House of Lords in November 2001.

Leading London human rights lawyer, Ms Chakrabarti, asked the European Court of Human Rights on Mrs Pretty's behalf, whether a terminally ill person could refuse life-saving or life-prolonging medical treatment and lawfully choose to commit suicide.

It was argued that the UK legislation on assisted suicide infringed Diane Pretty's human rights under Arts 2 of the European Convention ('right to life').

But the Strasbourg Court refused permission for assisted suicide, upholding the UK House of Lords' ruling, stating that Art. 2 was also there to protect life and that an intentional consensual killing in the context of 'voluntary euthanasia' was regarded in English law as murder.

Similarly, with abortion which is legalised. Whilst there are many groups who believe that euthanasia and abortion are immoral the law has moved differently.

Law and justice

Although justice is the main goal of the law it doesn't always provide a just outcome. There is the problem of defining justice as was outlined by Lord Wright, who said:

' the guiding principle of a judge in deciding cases is to do justice; that is justice according to the law, but still justice. I have not found any satisfactory definition of justice…what is just in a particular case is what appears just to the just man, in the same way as what is reasonable appears to be reasonable to the reasonable man'.

In many circumstances people's concepts of justice will be different. For example, the situation where a person uses force to repel a burglar and injures that person. This has been the cause of many a heated debate, from one end of the spectrum where it is thought right to be able to defend and kill in the process to the other end where it is seen as only right to defend but not injure. No doubt this debate will rage on forever more. This example highlights differing views on concepts of justice.

Rights and duties of individuals under the law

The law gives rights to individuals. It also gives methods of enforcing those rights if violated. The law also imposes duties on individuals. Rights and duties run through many areas such as contract and employment and also runs through criminal law, imposing a duty on the individual to obey the law and a right of the state to punish.

****

2

The Development of Law

The law in England and Wales has developed gradually over time. Law has been developed in a number of different ways, and the methods of developing law are known as sources of law. Historically, the most important ways were custom and decisions of judges. Parliament became more powerful in the eighteenth and nineteenth centuries, with Acts of Parliament becoming the main source of new laws, although judicial decisions were, and are, still important. During the twentieth century, statute law and judicial decisions continued to be the main sources of law, but increasingly two new sources of law became important: delegated legislation and European legislation. Together, all these sources of law have combined to create the present day legal system.

Customs

Customs are rules of behaviour which develop in a community. There are two main types of custom: general and local customs.

General customs

General customs are common customs which have developed and have been absorbed over time into law.

Local customs

Local customs is a term used where a person claims that he or she is entitled to some local right, such as a right of way or the right to use land in a certain way, because this is what has happened locally over time. Judge have a test of what constitutes local customs. These are as follows:

- The custom must have existed since 'time immemorial
- The custom must have been exercised peaceably openly and as of right
- The custom must be definite as to locality, nature and scope
- The custom must be reasonable

It is very rare for a new custom to be considered by courts nowadays. There have been certain exceptions. For example, in Egerton v Harding (1974) the court decided that there was a customary duty to fence land against cattle straying from the common. Although customs develop they are not part of the law until recognised by the courts.

Common law

The legal system historically could not rely on customs alone. In Anglo-Saxon times there were local courts that decided disputes but it was not until after the Norman conquest in 1066 that a more organised system of courts developed. Norman kings realised that control of the country was that much easier if the legal system was also controlled. William the Conqueror set up the Curia Regis (The Kings Court) and appointed judges to hear disputes from the nobles. In addition to this central court, judges were sent to major towns to decide important cases.

In the time of Henry 11 (1154-89) these tours became more regular and the country was divided up into circuits, or areas for the judges to visit. Initially the judges would use the local customs or the old Anglo-Saxon laws to decide cases. On return to London the judges would discuss customs and gradually these evolved into a uniform or common law.

Common law is the basis of our law today, an unwritten law that developed from customs and judicial decisions. The phrase 'common law' is still used to distinguish laws that have been developed by judicial decisions, from laws that have been created by statute or other legislation. For example murder is a common law crime whilst theft is a statutory crime.

Common law also has another meaning. It is used to distinguish between rules that were developed by the common law courts (the Kings Courts) and the rules of equity which were developed by the Lord Chancellor and the Chancery Courts.

Equity

Historically this is an important source still playing a part today with many of our legal concepts having developed from equitable principles. The word 'equity' has a meaning of fairness and this is the basis on which it operates.

Equity developed because of problems in the common law. Only certain types of cases were recognised. The law was also very technical; if there was an error in the formalities the person making the claim would lose the case. People who could not obtain justice in the common law courts appealed to the King. Most of these cases were referred to the Kings Chancellor. This was because the Chancellor based his decisions on principles of natural justice and fairness, making a decision on what seemed right in a particular case as opposed to the strict following of previous precedents. Account was also taken of what the parties had originally intended.

To ensure that decisions were fair, new procedures were introduced such as subpoenas, which ordered a witness to attend court. New remedies for compensation were developed which were able to compensate plaintiffs more fully than those previously used. The main equitable remedies were: injunctions; specific performance; rescission and rectification. These are all still in use today and will be explained more fully later on in this book.

Judicial precedents

The doctrine of precedents

Judicial precedent refers to the source of law where decisions of judges in the past create law for future judges to follow. This source of law is also known as case law and is a major source of law.

The English system of precedent is based on the Latin maxim *stare decisis et non quieta movere* which is usually shortened to *stare decisis* and which translated means 'stand by what has been decided and do not unsettle the established'. This supports the idea of fairness and certainty in law.

Ratio Decidendi

Precedent is only relevant and can only be effective if the reasons for past decisions are known. Judges will outline reasons for decisions and the rationale for a judgement outlining the principles of law used. These principles are an important part of any judgement and are known as the *ratio decidendi* which means the reason for deciding. This is what creates the precedent for future judges to follow.

Obiter Dicta

The remainder of the judgement is called *obiter dicta* (other things said) and judges in future cases do not have to follow it.

Original precedent

If the point of law in a case has never been decided before, then whatever the judge decides will form a new precedent for future cases to follow. As there are no past cases for a judge to base his decision on, he is likely to look at cases which are the closest in principle and he may decide to use similar rules. This way of arriving at a judgement is called reasoning by analogy. The idea of creating new law by analogy can be seen in Hunter and others v Canary Wharf Limited and London Docklands Development Corporation (1995). Part of the decision involved whether the interference with television reception was capable of constituting an actionable private nuisance. The facts of the case were that the main tower Canary Wharf built in the Isle of Dogs East London, was 250 metres high and 50 metres square. The claimant and others claimed damages from the defendant for continuing interference over a number of years with the television reception in the area as a result of the height of the tower.

In the Court of Appeal, the Lord Justice Pill stated:

'Lord Irving (counsel for the defendants) submits that interference with television reception by reason of the presence of a building is properly to be regarded as analogous to loss of aspect (view). To obstruct the receipt of television signals by the erection of a building between the point of receipt and the source is not in law a nuisance............... I accept the importance of television in the lives of people. However, in my judgement the erection or presence of a building in the line of sight between a television transmitter and other properties is not actionable as an interference with the use and enjoyment of land. The analogy with loss of prospect is compelling. The loss of a view, which may be of the greatest importance to householders, is not actionable and neither is the mere presence of a building in the site lines to the television transmitter'.

Binding precedent

This is a precedent from an earlier case which must be followed even if the judge in the later case does not agree with the principle. A binding precedent is only created where the facts of the second case are sufficiently similar to the original case.

Persuasive precedent

This is a precedent that is not binding on the court but the judge may consider it and decide that it is a correct principle and is persuaded that it should be followed. Persuasive precedent comes from a number of sources:

- Courts lower in the hierarchy
- Decisions by the Judicial Committee of the Privy Council
- Statements made obiter dicta
- A dissenting judgement
- Decisions of courts in foreign countries.

The hierarchy of courts and precedent

In England and Wales courts operate a rigid hierarchy of judicial precedents. Every court is bound to follow any decision made by a court above it in the hierarchy. In general, appellate courts (appeal courts) are bound by their own decisions. The diagram below indicates the hierarchy of courts.

See overleaf.

HIERARCHY OF COURTS

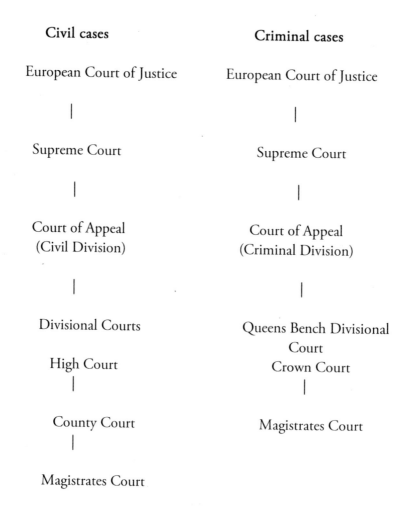

Civil cases	Criminal cases
European Court of Justice	European Court of Justice
|	|
Supreme Court	Supreme Court
|	|
Court of Appeal (Civil Division)	Court of Appeal (Criminal Division)
|	|
Divisional Courts	Queens Bench Divisional Court
High Court	Crown Court
|	|
County Court	Magistrates Court
|	
Magistrates Court	

HM Courts & Tribunals Service

HM Courts & Tribunals Service was created on 1 April 2011. It brings together HM Courts Service & Tribunals Service into one integrated agency providing support for the administration of justice in courts and tribunals.

HM Courts & Tribunals Service is an agency of the Ministry of Justice. It uniquely operates as a partnership between the Lord Chancellor, the Lord Chief Justice and the Senior President of Tribunals as set out in our Framework Document.

The agency is responsible for the administration of the criminal, civil and family courts and tribunals in England and Wales and non-devolved tribunals in Scotland and Northern Ireland. It provides for a fair, efficient and effective justice system delivered by an independent judiciary.

HM Courts & Tribunals Service aims to ensure that all citizens receive timely access to justice according to their different needs, whether as victims or witnesses of crime, defendants accused of crimes, consumers in debt, children at risk of harm, businesses involved in commercial disputes or as individuals asserting their employment rights or challenging the decisions of government bodies.

About Tribunals

Tribunals are specialist judicial bodies which decide disputes in particular areas of law.

Appeals to tribunals are generally against a decision made by a Government department or agency. The exception to this is the Employment Tribunal where cases are on a party v party basis (i.e. employee versus employer).

There are tribunals in England, Wales, Scotland and Northern Ireland covering a wide range of areas affecting day-to-day life. HM Courts & Tribunals administers many of them although some are the responsibility of the devolved governments in Scotland, Wales and Northern Ireland.

Appeals to the First-tier Tribunal are against the decisions from government departments and other public bodies. The Upper Tribunal hears appeals from the First-tier Tribunal on points of law i.e. an appeal made over the interpretation of a legal principle or statute. Further appeals may be made, with permission, to the Court of Appeal.

Tribunal judges are legally-qualified. Tribunal members are specialist non-legal members of the panel and include doctors, chartered surveyors, ex-service personnel or accountants. Tribunals often sit as a panel comprising a judge and non-legal members however in some jurisdictions cases may be heard by a judge or member sitting alone.

Tribunals adopt procedures that are less complicated and more informal than those typically associated with the courts.

The European Court of Justice

The highest court affecting the legal system in England and Wales is the European Court of Justice. This has been the case since 1973. For points of European law, a decision made by this court is binding on all other courts in England and Wales. There are still laws unaffected by European Union law and for these the House of Lords is the supreme court.

Supreme Court

The Supreme Court of the United Kingdom
The Supreme Court of the United Kingdom was established by the Constitutional Reform Act of 2005. The Court started work on October 1st 2009. It has taken over the judicial functions of the House of Lords, which were exercised by the Lords of Appeal in Ordinary Law (Law Lords), the 12 professional judges appointed as members of the House of Lords to carry out its judicial business. It also assumes some functions of the Judicial Committee of the Privy Council.

The court is the Supreme Court (court of last resort, highest appellate court) in all matters under English law, Welsh law (to the extent that the National Assembly for Wales makes laws for Wales that differ from those in England) and Northern Irish law. It does not have authority over criminal cases in Scotland, where the High Court of Justiciary remains the supreme criminal court. However, it will hear appeals from the civil court of session, just as the House of Lords did before.

Court of appeal

The court of appeal is next in the hierarchy and has two divisions, civil and criminal. Both of these divisions are bound to follow the decisions of the European Court of Justice and the Supreme Court. They must also follow past decisions of their own although there are exceptions to the rule and the Court of Appeal (Criminal Division) is more flexible where it involves the liberty of the subject.

Divisional courts

The three divisional courts, Queens bench, Chancery and Family are bound by decisions of the European Court of Justice, the Supreme Court and the Court of Appeal. The divisional courts are also bound by their own past decisions, although there are some exceptions.

Courts of first instance

This term means any court where the original trial of a case is held. Appeal courts do not hear any original trials only appeals from those trials. Courts of first instance rarely ever create precedents only following decisions of courts above them.

The High Court

The High Court is bound by decisions of all courts above it and in turn it binds the lower courts.

Inferior courts

Inferior courts are the Crown Court, the County Court and the Magistrates Court. They are bound to follow decisions of all higher courts. It is very unlikely that a decision by a lower court can create a precedent. The one exception is that a ruling on a point of law by a judge in a Crown Court will bind the Magistrates Court.

Use of Practice Statement

Until 1966, the House of Lords in the United Kingdom was bound to follow all of its previous decisions under the principle of *stare decisis*, even if this created "injustice" and "unduly restrict(s) the proper development of the law" (London Tramways Co. v London County Council [1898] AC 375). The **Practice Statement** 1966 is authority for the House of Lords to depart from their previous decisions. It does not affect the precedential value of cases in lower courts; all other courts that recognise the Supreme Court (formerly the House of Lords)as the [court of last resort] are still bound by Supreme Court decisions. Before this, the only way a binding precedent could be avoided was to create new legislation on the matter.

Distinguishing, overruling and reversing previous decisions

Distinguishing is a method used by a judge to avoid following a past decision which otherwise would have to be followed. It means that the judge finds that the material facts of the case he is following are sufficiently different for him to draw a distinction between the present case and the previous case. He is not then bound by the previous case. Overruling is where a court in a later case decides that the legal rule in a previous case is wrong. Overruling may occur when a higher court overrules a decision by a lower court, for example the Supreme Court overruling a decision by the Court of Appeal.

Reversing is where a court higher up in the hierarchy overturns the decision of a lower court on appeal in the same case.

Advantages and disadvantages of precedent in the law

There are advantages and disadvantages to the way judicial precedent operates in England and Wales.

Advantages

The main advantages to the operation of precedent are:

Certainty
Because the courts follow past decisions, people know what the law is and how it is likely to be applied in their case. Lawyers advise clients on the likely outcome of cases and it also allows people to operate their businesses in the certainty that what they do is within the law.

Consistency and fairness
It is seen as just and fair that similar cases are decided in the same way.

Precision
As the principles of law are set out in actual cases, the law becomes very precise.

Flexibility
There is room for the law to change as the Supreme Court can use the Practice Statement to overrule cases.

Time- saving
Precedent can be considered a useful time saving device as where a principle has been established, cases with similar facts are unlikely to go through the lengthy process of litigation.

Disadvantages

Rigidity

The fact that lower courts have to follow decisions of higher courts, together with the fact that the Court of Appeal has to follow its own past decisions, can make the law too inflexible so that bad decisions made in the past can be perpetuated.

Complexity

There are many reported cases and it may be complex and time consuming to find the right case on which to base a decision.

Illogical distinctions

The use of distinguishing to avoid past decisions can lead to illogical distinctions so that some areas of law have become very complex.

Reporting cases

Written law reports have existed in England and Wales since the 13th century. Reports right from the early times were inaccurate and difficult to follow. In 1865 the Incorporated Council of Law was set up, controlled by the courts. Law reports became more accurate and precise, with judgements being noted word for word. This accuracy of reports was one of the factors in the development of the strict doctrine of precedent. There are also other well established reports today, notably the All England Series (abbreviated to All ER) and the weekly law Reports (WLR). The internet also provides reports, websites such as www.parliament.uk and www. lawreports.co.uk.

3

Parliament and Acts of Parliament

The main legislative body in the United Kingdom is Parliament. Laws passed by Parliament are known as Acts of Parliament, or statutes. This source of law is usually referred to as statute law. In addition to Parliament, power is delegated to government ministers and their departments to make detailed rules and regulations which supplement Parliament. These regulations are delegated legislation and are called statutory instruments.

Parliament consists of the House of Commons and the House of Lords. Both houses must be in favour of a bill, vote in its favour, before it can become law.

The people who sit in the House of Commons are elected Members of Parliament, representing their constituencies who elected them.

The House of Lords is somewhat different consisting of hereditary peers, life peers, judges who are law lords and the most senior bishops in the Church of England. The Lords has, in the past few years, undergone radical reform with the process still continuing. Essentially, the process whereby hereditary peers dominated the Lords has ended with a more democratic approach being sought.

Judges in the Supreme Court

As discussed, the Supreme Court is the most senior court in England and Wales. Only the 12 Law Lords are allowed to sit in this court

Factors influencing law making at a government level

When they are formed, Governments have programmes of reforms. These are set out in government manifestos at election time and reinforced during the Queens speech at the opening of Parliament. Basically, most new legislation emanates from government policy.

There are other influences at play which affect what laws are enacted. One such major influence is European legislation. New Acts are passed to bring our law in line with European legislation. Other outside influences include proposals for law reform put forward by law reform agencies, commissions or enquiries into the effectiveness of existing law. Specific events can also lead to changes in the law, events such as the massacre of young children at a school in Dunblane in 1996 which resulted in Firearms Legislation in 1997. Another outside influence is that of pressure groups who cause government to reconsider law in specific areas. One such instance was in 1994 when the government reduced the age of homosexual consent from 21 to 18. In 2000, this was further reduced to 16.

The pre-legislative process

On major matters a minister with responsibility for a specific area will issue a Green paper. This is a consultative document on a topic with the government's views on law reform. Following receipt of the views of all interested parties a White Paper will then be issued with its firm proposals for new law.

Introducing an Act of Parliament

The majority of Acts of Parliament are introduced by the government of the day. They are initially drafted by civil service lawyers known as Parliamentary Counsel to the Treasury. When the proposed Act has been drafted it is published as a Bill. It will only progress to become an Act of Parliament if it completes all the stages successfully in

Parliament. The drafting of Bills is painstaking and exact and must be framed in terms which are unambiguous. This is against a backdrop of the inevitable pressure of time.

Bills can also be sponsored by individual MP's. The Parliamentary process allows for a ballot in each session in which 20 private members are selected who can then take their turn in presenting a Bill to Parliament. Time for debate of these Bills is limited, usually being debated on a Friday and only a few members have a realistic chance of introducing a Bill on their chosen topic. Only a few Private Members Bills become law. Notable Acts passed have been the Abortion Act of 1967 which legalised abortion and the Marriage Act 1994 which allowed marriage in any registered place.

Backbenchers can also try to introduce a Bill through what is known as the 'Ten Minute Rule' under which any MP can make a speech of up to 10 minutes supporting the introduction of new legislation.

Members of the House of Lords can also introduce Private Members Bills.

The distinction between public and private Bills

A public Bill involves matters of public policy which will affect the country at large or a significant section of the country. Most Government Bills are in this category. However, some Bills are passed aimed at individuals or companies which are private Bills.

The Parliamentary process

In order for a Bill to become an Act of Parliament, it will usually have to be passed by both House of Commons and House of Lords. In each House there is a long process. A bill may commence in either House with the exception of finance Bills which must commence in the

Commons. There are a number of stages which all Bills must go through to become law:

1. First reading

This is a formal procedure where the name and aims of the Bill are read out. There will be a vote on whether the House wants to consider the Bill further. The vote can be verbal, where the speaker of the House asks the members as a whole how they vote and they shout out 'Aye' or 'No'. If it is clear that all members are in agreement, either for or against then there is no need for a formal vote. If it is not clear then a formal vote will be taken. Members of the House will leave the Chamber and then re-enter by one of two doors signifying for or against. Tellers total the votes for and against and declare the result to the Speaker.

2. Second reading

The second reading is the main debate on the whole Bill in which MP's debate the principles underlying the Bill. No one may speak without being called on to do so by the Speaker. At the end of the process a vote is taken in the same way as the first reading. To proceed to the next stage the Bill must be voted in favour of.

3. Committee stage

This stage is where a detailed examination of the Bill is undertaken by a committee of between 16 and 50 MP's. This is called a Standing Committee which is a committee chosen specifically to examine the Bill. This committee is made up by opposition and minority parties as well as the Government who will have a majority. Membership is made up in direct proportion to parties seats in the Houses of Parliament and will consist of people with a knowledge of the matter in hand.

4. Report stage

At the Committee stage amendments to various clauses in the Bill may have been voted on and passed. The report stage is where the Committee reports back to the House on the amendments.

5. Third reading

This stage is the final vote on the Bill. Having reached this stage it is unlikely to fail.

6. The House of Lords

If the Bill emanated from the Commons it will now go to the Lords where it will go through the same five stages and if amendments are made by the Lords to the Bill then it will go back to the Commons to consider those amendments. If the Bill emanated from the Lords then it will go to the Commons.

7. Royal assent

The final stage is where the monarch gives approval to the Bill and it then becomes an Act of Parliament. This is a formality. Under the Royal Assent Act 1961, the Monarch will not even have the text of Bills to which she is assenting. She will only have the title of the Bill. The diagram below summarises the process of legislation from drafting of a Bill to Act of Parliament through the House of Commons.

The Bill is Drafted

|

First reading in the House of Commons

|

Second reading in the House of Commons

|

Committee stage

|

Report stage

|

Third reading in the House of Commons

|

Same procedures in The House of Lords

|

Royal assent

The power of the House of Lords to reject a Bill is limited by the Parliament Acts of 1911 and 1949. These Acts allow a Bill to become law even if the Lords reject it provided that the Bill is re-introduced into the House of Commons in the next session of Parliament and goes through all the stages once again. The principle behind the Acts is that the House of Lords is not an elected body and its function is not to oppose the will of the elected House of Commons but to refine the law.

Commencement of an Act

Following Royal Assent the Act becomes law on midnight of that day, unless another date has been set for it to become law. This has become the norm, where a date is set where it should become law. A commencement order will be issued by the appropriate minister. In many cases, sections of an Act come into force at different times which causes confusion. This again is becoming something of a norm. One such Act was the Criminal Justice Act of 2003.

Parliamentary sovereignty

Parliamentary law is sovereign over other forms of law in England and Wales. This means that an Act of Parliament can completely supersede any custom, judicial precedent, delegated legislation or previous Act of Parliament. However, European law has undermined the sovereignty of Parliament in certain areas of law.

4

European Law

Recent history

Since January 1ˢᵗ 1973, when the United Kingdom joined what was then the European Economic Community, set up by the Treaty of Rome in 1957, European law has gained an ever greater significance. Currently, there are 28 member states (as at 2013) in the European Union. The European Union is a vast and complex organisation. Changes were made to the EU and European Institutions to cope with the EU's expanded membership through the intended passing of a new European Constitution. The constitution within Part 1 contained wide raging reforms, *inter alia*:

- Explicitly stating that EU law had priority over domestic law of Member States
- The constitution would be the highest form of law
- EU legal instruments would be reclassified to provide a clear hierarchy distinguishing between administrative and legislative forms
- The EU would have stronger political profile with the creation of a Commission President and Minister of Foreign Affairs
- The number of commissioners would be reduced to two-thirds the number of Member States
- The European parliament would be restricted to 750 members (now 766) and its legislative role would be increased
- The president of the European Council would be appointed for two and a half years rather than six months
- The system of voting within the European Council would be changed.

Part 2 of the European Constitution contained a Charter of Fundamental Rights. These provisions covered:

- civil rights
- political rights
- economic rights
- social rights.

However, voters in England and France rejected the European Constitution. As a result a treaty, signed in Lisbon in 2007, was drawn up to replace the draft European Constitution. The Lisbon Treaty was initially rejected by Irish voters in a referendum on 12th June 2008. Under EU rules, the treaty could not enter into force if any of the 27 member states failed to ratify it. The treaty was eventually ratified by all 27 Member States in November 2009 and came into force on December 1st 2009. The Lisbon Treaty was ratified in the UK on 19th June 2008 under the European Union Amendment Act 2008.

Whereas the Constitution attempted to replace all earlier EU treaties and start afresh, the new treaty merely amends the Treaty on European Union and the Treaty establishing the European Union without replacing them. It provides the Union with a legal framework and tools necessary to meet future challenges and respond to citizen demands. The Lisbon treaty contains many of the changes that the Constitution attempted to introduce.

The main institutions which exercise the functions of the EU are:

- The Council of the European Union
- The Commission of the EU
- The Council of Ministers
- The European Parliament
- The European Court of Justice
- The European Central Bank

There are a number of ancillary bodies, the Economic and Social Committee being the most important.

The Council of Ministers

The government of each nation in the EU will send a representative to the Council. Usually the minister responsible for a particular area under discussion will attend. Twice a year, government heads meet in the European Council or Summit to discuss matters of policy. The member states take it in turns to provide the President of the Council, each for a six-month period. To assist with the day-to-day work of the council there is a committee of permanent representatives known as the *coreper.*

The Commission

The Commission consists of up to 30 Commissioners who are supposed to act independently. They are appointed for a five-year term and will head a specific department during their tenure. The Commission has several functions, proposing policies and presenting drafts of legislation to the Council. The Commission is also the 'guardian' of treaties. It ensures that treaty provisions adopted by the Council are properly implemented. It is also responsible for the administration of the Union.

The Assembly

The Assembly advises the Council and the Commission on economic matters. It is made up of representatives of influential interest groups such as farmers, employees and manufacturers. The Assembly must be consulted on proposed Union measures and has considerable influence on the decision making process.

The Court of Justice of the European Union

The Court of Justice of the European Union consists of three courts:

- The European Court of Justice (The ECJ)
- The General Court
- Civil Service Tribunal

The European Court of Justice

The court of primary importance is the European Court of Justice. The function of the European Court of Justice is set out in Article 220 of the Treaty of Rome. This states that ' the Court must ensure that in the interpretation and application of the treaty the law is observed'.

The Court sits in Luxembourg and has 27 judges, one from each member state. Each judge is appointed for a term of six years and can be further reappointed. The Court is assisted by nine Advocates General who are also appointed for six years. Each case brought before the EU Court of Justice is given to an Advocates General whose task is to research all the appropriate legal points and to present a reasoned conclusion on cases to the Court.

The Courts main task is to ensure that the law is applied uniformly in all member states. It will hear cases to decide whether member states have failed to fulfil obligations under the Treaties. Such actions are usually initiated by the European Commission, although they can be started by another Member State.

The Court will also hear references from national courts for preliminary rulings on points of European law. Rulings made by the European Court of Justice are then binding on all Member States. This ensures that the law is uniform throughout Member States.

A request for a preliminary ruling is made under Article 234 of the Treaty of Rome. This states:

'the Court of Justice shall have jurisdiction to give preliminary rulings concerning:

a) *the interpretation of Treaties;*
b) *the validity and interpretation of Acts of the Institution of the Union;*
c) *the interpretation of the statutes of bodies established by an Act of the Council, where those statutes so provide.*

Article 234 goes on to state that where there is no appeal from the national court within the national system, then courts must refer points of European law to the European Court of justice.

If this is applied to the court system in England and Wales, this means that the Supreme Court must refer questions of European law, as it is the highest appeal court in our legal system. However, the Court of Appeal does not have to refer questions.

However, even courts at the bottom of the system can refer questions of law under Article 234 if they feel that a preliminary ruling is necessary to enable a judgement in a particular case to be given. The European Court will not decide such a case only make a preliminary ruling and then refer the case back to the court in question.

Discretionary referrals

The Court of Appeal set out its approach to discretionary referrals in the case of Bulmer v Bollinger (1974). The guidelines are as follows:

- Guidance on a point of law must be necessary to come to a decision in a case
- There is no need to refer a question which has already been decided by the European Union in a previous case
- There is no need to refer a point which is reasonably clear and free from doubt
- The court must consider all the circumstances of the case

- The English court retains the discretion on whether to refer or not

The Court of First Instance

This was set up in 1988 to relieve the European Court of Justice of some of its workload. It is now known as the General Court following changes made by the Lisbon Treaty. In addition, a Civil Service Tribunal hears cases between European institutions and their employees.

The Lisbon Treaty also officially recognised the European Central Bank based in Germany as an institution of the European union. It is responsible for organising and co-ordinating both the monetary and economic policy of the Member States of the European Union that have adopted the Euro, the single European Currency. It is independently responsible for keeping inflation under control and setting interest rates within the Eurozone.

Regulations

Under Article 249 of the Treaty of Rome, the European Union has the power to issue regulations which are binding in every respect and directly applicable to every Member state. Such regulations do not have to be adopted by Member States as they automatically become law in each member country.

Directives

Directives are the main way in which harmonisation of laws within Member states is achieved. There have been directives covering a whole range of topics, such as company law, banking, insurance employment and consumer law. As with regulations, Article 249 of the Treaty of Rome gives the power to the Union to issue directives. Article 249 states directives:

'bind any Member state to which they are addressed as to the result to be achieved, while leaving to domestic agencies a competence as to form and means'

This means that Member states will pass their own laws to bring directives into effect. The usual method of implementing directives in the United Kingdom is by Statutory Instrument. One key example of this was the Unfair Terms in Consumer Contracts Regulations 1994. The time-frame for implementation is set by the European Commission.

Where Member states have not implemented a directive within the time set out by the Commission, the European Court of Justice has developed the concept of 'direct effect'. This means that a directive may be directly enforceable by an individual or by a member state. This will be the case even though a Member state has not implemented the directive or has implemented it incorrectly. The main point here is that the individual who is affected only has rights against the state. This is because of the concepts of vertical and horizontal effect.

Vertical effect
Vertical direct effect was illustrated effectively in the case of Marshall v Southampton and South West Area health Authority (1986). The facts were that Miss Marshall was required to retire from her post at the age of 62. Men doing the same work did not have to retire until the age of 65. Under the Sex Discrimination Act 1976 in English Law, this was not discriminatory. However, Miss Marshall succeeded in her action for unfair dismissal by relying on the Equal Treatment Directive 76/207. This directive had not been fully implemented in the United Kingdom but the European Court of Justice held that it was sufficiently clear and imposed obligations on a Member State. This ruling allowed Miss Marshall to succeed in her action against her employers because they were an arm of the state, i.e. they were considered as part of the state. The directive had vertical effect allowing

her to rely on it to take action against them. The concept of state is quite wide, as it was ruled by the European Court of Justice in Foster v British Gas plc (1990) that the state was:

'a body, whatever its legal form, which has been made responsible, pursuant to a measure adopted by the State, for providing a public service under the control of the State and has for that purpose special powers beyond those which result from the normal rules applicable in relations between individuals'.

Horizontal direct effect

Directives which have not been implemented do not give an individual any rights against other people. As seen they are only applicable in cases against the state.

The conflict between European law and national law

Inevitably there will be conflict between national and European law. European law takes precedence over national law. This was first established in Van Gend en Loos (1963) which involved a conflict of Dutch law and European law on customs duty. The Dutch Government argued that the European Court of Justice had no jurisdiction to decide whether European law would prevail over Dutch law. However, the European Court rejected this argument. In Costa v ENEL (1964) the European Court decided that even if there was a later national law this did not take precedence over EU law.

5

Statutory Interpretation of the Law

In many cases, there are disputes over the meaning of Acts of Parliament. Although Acts will have interpretive sections allowing for broader interpretations of the Act there is, in many cases, still confusion.

In cases such as the above it is the courts role to interpret the Act and decide the exact meaning of a particular word, group of words or a phrase. The reasons why a meaning can be unclear are many and include the fact that broad terms have been used to cover several possibilities, there is ambiguity, error in drafting, new developments rendering older Acts of Parliament obsolete, changes in the use of language and so on. For all these reasons and more, sometimes the courts are called on to interpret an Act.

Literal approach versus Purposive approach

One of the major problems concerning statutory interpretation is that of whether the judge in a case should take each word in an Act and interpret it literally or whether he/she should go beyond the literal meaning and take a more purposive approach, accept that words cannot cover all situations and look at the facts of the case more closely. In English law judges have not been able to agree on which approach to adopt. However, over the years they have developed three different rules of interpretation:

- The literal rule
- The golden rule
- The mischief rule

We will discuss each one in turn.

The literal rule

Under this rule courts will give words their plain, ordinary or literal meaning, even if the end result of such an interpretation is undesirable and not very sensible. This idea was expressed by Lord Esher in R v Judge of the City of London Court (1892) when he said:

' *if the words of an Act are clear then you must follow them even though they lead to a manifest absurdity. The court has nothing to do with the question whether the legislature has committed an absurdity'.*

The rule above has been used since the early nineteenth century and in many cases the outcome has been nonsense.

The golden rule

This rule is a modification of the literal rule. The golden rule starts by looking at the literal meaning but the court is then allowed to arrive at an interpretation which avoids absurdity.

The mischief rule

This rule gives the judge more discretion than the literal or golden rules. The definition of the mischief rule comes from the Heydon's case (1584) where it was said that there were four points the court should consider. These (couched in the original language) were:

1. What was the common law before the making of the Act?
2. What was the mischief and defect for which the common law did not provide?
3. What was the remedy the Parliament hath resolved and appointed to cure the disease of the commonwealth?
4. The true reason of the remedy.

Then the office of all judges is always to make such construction as shall suppress the mischief and advance the remedy.

Under this rule therefore, the court should look to see what the law was before the Act was passed in order to discover what gap, or 'mischief' the Act was intended to cover. The court should then interpret the Act in such a way that the gap is covered.

Rules of language

Even the literal rule does not take cases in complete isolation. Other words in the Act must be looked at to see if they affect the word or phrase which is in dispute. In looking at other words the courts have developed a set of rules:

- The *ejusdem generis* rule
- The express mention of one thing excludes others
- A word is known by the company it keeps

The *ejusdem generis* rule

This rule states that where there is a list of words followed by general words, then the general words are limited to the same kind of items as the specific words. If we look at the case of *Powell v Kempton park Racecourse* (1899) the defendant was charged with 'keeping a house, an office, room or other place for betting'. He had been operating betting at what was known as Tattersall's Ring, which is outside. The court decided that the general words 'other place' had to refer to

49

indoor places since all words in the list were indoor places so the defendant was not guilty.

There must be at least two specific words in a list for this rule to operate.

Expressio Unius Exclusio Alterius (the mention of one thing excludes others

Where there is a list of words which is not followed by general words, then the Act applies only to the items in the list. In *Tempest v Kilner* (1846) the court had to consider whether the Statute of Frauds 1677 (which required a contract for the sale of goods, wares and merchandise, of more than £10 to be evidenced in writing) applied to a contract for the sale of stocks and shares. The list 'goods, wares and merchandise, was not followed by any general words, so the court decided that only contracts for three types of things were affected by the statute: because the stocks and shares were not mentioned they were not caught by the statute.

NOSCITUR A SOCIIS (a word is known by the company it keeps)

This means that the words must be looked at in context and interpreted accordingly. It involves looking at words in the same section or other section of the Act. One case which illustrates this is *Inland Revenue Commissioners v Frere* (1965) where the section set out rules for 'interest, annuities or other annual interest'. The first use of the word 'interest' on its own could have meant any interest paid, whether daily, monthly or annually. Because of the words 'other annual interest' in the section, the court decided that 'interest' only meant annual interest.

Presumptions

The courts will also make certain presumptions about the law. If the statute clearly states the opposite, then the presumption will not apply and it is said that the presumption is rebutted. The most important presumptions are: a presumption against a change in the common law, i.e. a presumption that the common law has not changed unless Parliament has changed it in an Act; a presumption that *mens rea* is required in a criminal case. The basic common law rule is that no-one can be convicted of a crime unless it is shown that they had the intention to commit it.

There will also be a presumption that the Crown is not bound by any statute unless the statute expressly says so. There will be a presumption that legislation does not apply retrospectively.

Unified approach to interpretation

Looking at all these approaches the question is raised, how do they all fit together. The unified approach, according to Sir Rupert Cross, is thus:

1. A judge should start by using the grammatical and ordinary or, where appropriate, technical meaning of the words in the general context of the statute.
2. If the judge considers that this would produce an absurd result, then he may apply any secondary meaning, which the words are capable of bearing.
3. The judge may read in words which he considers to be necessarily implied by the words which are in the statute, and he has a limited power to add to, alter or ignore words in order to prevent a provision from being unintelligible, unworkable or absurd.
4. In applying these rules the judge may resort to the various aids and presumptions.

The purposive approach

Using this approach, judges will decide what they believe Parliament meant to achieve. The major exponent of this approach was Lord Denning. In the case of Magor and St Mellons v Newport Corporation (1950) he said:

' *We sit here to find out the intention of Parliament and carry it out, and we do this better by filling in the gaps and making sense of the enactment than by opening it up to destructive analysis'.*

There have been many criticisms of the purposive approach, with judges stating that it is up to the courts not to interpret legislation but to follow the enactment. If any amendments need to be made they should be made by amending the Act.

6

The Legal Profession

In the English Legal System, there are two types of lawyers, Barristers and Solicitors.

The Law Society oversees the activities of solicitors as well as the legal profession as a whole. The General Council of the Bar oversees Barristers.

The Legal Services Act 2007

This Act created a new regulatory structure, the objects of which are:

- Protecting and promoting public interests
- Supporting the rule of law
- Improving access to justice
- Protecting consumer interests
- Promoting competition in legal services
- Encouraging an independent, strong, diverse and effective legal professions
- Increasing public understanding of citizen's rights and duties
- Promoting professional principles

All the representatives and regulatory bodies described below are under a duty to promote these objects.

The Legal Services Board (LSB) and the Legal Ombudsman

The LSB was created by the 2007 Act to oversee the eight bodies regulating different types of lawyer, including solicitors. The Legal

Ombudsman was created under the Act, in 2010, and is a free complaints service about the main categories of lawyer or legal service provider: barristers, law costs draftsmen, legal executives, licensed conveyancers, notaries, patent attorneys, probate practitioners, registered European lawyers, solicitors and trade mark lawyers.

Solicitors

The Law Society

This is the trade union of solicitors, to " help, protect and promote solicitors across England and wales. It used to be the professional regulatory body but it lost this function under the 2007 Act.

The Solicitors Regulation Authority

This is the professional governing body of solicitors, regulating their training, discipline and standards of professional conduct. It can fine individuals and law firms and/or apply conditions to their authorisation and refer them to the Solicitors Disciplinary Tribunal, which can levy unlimited fines.

The Office of Legal Complaints

Since 2010, this impartial body handles complaints. The function was removed from the Law Society in 2010.

Solicitors generally

In 2001, there were 159, 524 solicitors on the role. To become a solicitor it is usual to either have a law degree or have completed an extra year of law if the degree is a non-law degree. This is called the Common Professional Examination.

When the course has been completed successfully the student is still not a solicitor. A training contract must be obtained from a firm of solicitors and two years work must be completed. This training period can also be undertaken in other legal organisations such as the Crown Prosecution Service, or the legal department of a local authority. During the training period he or she will have to undertake their own work and complete a 20 day Professional Skills Course after which time the person will be admitted as a solicitor by the Law Society. Even after qualifying, solicitors have to attend continuing education to keep their skills up to date.

There is a non-graduate route to become a solicitor for mature candidates but the process takes longer to complete.

Solicitors who qualify will either work in private practice in a solicitors firm, or can work for the Crown Prosecution Service or for a local authority or government department. Some will become legal advisors to big companies.

Solicitors will work in sole practices or partnerships and the type of work carried out will be varied depending largely on the specialism of the firm. A small firm will usually cover a whole range of matters from housing, family, conveyancing and business matters. It is usual for a solicitor to specialise in a particular area.

All solicitors can act as advocates in the Magistrates Court. After 1986 solicitors can appear in a High Court to make a statement after a case has been settled.

Barristers

In 2010, there were 15, 378 barristers with a practising certificate, 80 per cent of whom were in private practice.

The Bar Council

The General Council of the Bar represents the interests of barristers. It was their professional governing body but lost that function to the Bar Standards Board in advance of the LSA 2007. The six court circuits have their own Bar Associations, as do specialist barristers.

The Inns of Court

Each barrister must belong to an Inn of Court: Gray's inn, Lincolns inn, Inner Temple or Middle Temple.

The Bar Standards Board

This was created in 2006, anticipating the LSA 2007, taking over enforcement of professional standards and enforcing the Bar's Code of Conduct. It handles complaints and is subject to oversight by the LSB.

Professional liability

In 2000, in Arthur J Hall (a firm) v Simons, the House of Lords held that barristers and other advocates, including solicitors, could be sued for negligence in their conduct of civil and criminal proceedings. This reversed the rule in Rondel v Worsley (1969).

Entry to the Bar is usually degree based although a small number of mature entrants can qualify. As with solicitor's graduates with a non-law degree can take a one-year course for the Common Professional Examination in the core subjects in order to qualify as a barrister. All student barristers must pass the Bar Vocational Course which emphasises the practical skills of drafting pleadings for use in court negotiation and advocacy.

All student barristers must join one of the four Inns of Court. Until 1997 it was mandatory to dine there 12 times before being called to the Bar. However, students may now attend in a different way, such as a weekend residential course.

After being called to the Bar a Barrister must complete a practical stage of the training called pupillage. This is on-the-job training where the trainee barrister becomes a pupil to a qualified barrister. This involves shadowing the barrister and can be with the same barrister for 12 months or with two barristers for six months each. There is also a requirement to take part in ongoing continuing education organised by the Bar Council. After the first six months of pupillage barristers can appear on their own in court.

Barristers practicing at the Bar are self-employed but share the administrative expenses of a set of chambers. Most sets of chambers comprise 15-29 barristers. They will employ a clerk as an administrator. The majority of barristers will concentrate on advocacy, although there are some who will specialise.

Originally, it was necessary for anyone who wanted to instruct a barrister to go to a solicitor first. The solicitor would then brief the barrister. After September 2004, it has been possible for anyone to contact barristers direct. However, direct access is still not allowed for criminal work or family work.

Barristers can be employed direct (the employed bar) working for example, for the Crown Prosecution Service and can represent in court.

Queen's Counsel

After a Barrister or solicitor has served at least 16 years with an advocacy qualification, it is then possible to become a Queens Counsel (QC). About 10% of the Bar are Queens Counsel and it is known as 'taking silk'. QC's usually take on complicated, high profile cases. Until 2004 Queen's Counsel were appointed by the Lord Chancellor.

After 2004, selection is by a panel chaired by a non-lawyer. Selection is by interview and applicants can provide references.

Solicitors and barristers summarised

	Solicitors	Barristers
Professional body	Law Society	Bar Council
Basic qualifications	Law degree or non-law degree with one years Common Professional Exam	Law degree or non-law degree with one years Common Professional Exam
Vocational training	Legal practice course	Bar vocational course
Practical training	Training contract	Pupillage
Methods of working	Firm of partners or sole practitioner	Self-employed Practicing in Chambers
Rights of audience	Normally only County Court and Magistrates Court	All courts
Relationship with client	Contractual	Normally through solicitor but Accountants and Surveyors can Brief barristers Directly
Liability	Liable in contract and tort to clients may also be liable to others affected by negligence	No contractual liability but liable for negligence

Legal executives and paralegals

Much of the everyday work of solicitor's offices is performed by legal executives, paralegals with specialist qualifications. The Chartered

Institute of Legal Executives (CILEX) is their representative body. They can become partners in a legal disciplinary practice and gain advocacy rights and also become district judges.

The Judiciary

Collectively, judges are known as the judiciary. The head of the Judiciary is the Lord Chancellor.

Types of judges

Superior judges

Superior judges are those in the high court and above. These are (from top to bottom):

- The 12 justices of the Supreme Court
- The Lords Justices of Appeal in the Court of Appeal
- Master of the Rolls (Court of Appeal Civil Division)
- Lord Justice of Appeal-Court of Appeal
- High Court Judges (known as puisne judges) who sit in the three divisions of the High Court

Specific posts heading the different divisions of the Court of Appeal and the High Court are:

- The Lord Chief Justice, who is the president of the Criminal Division of the Court of Appeal and the senior judge in the Queens Bench Division of the High Court
- The Master of the Rolls who is president of the Civil Division of the Court of Appeal
- The President of the Family Division of the High Court
- The Vice Chancellor of the Chancery Division of the High Court

Inferior judges

The inferior judges are:

- Circuit judges who sit in both the Crown Court and the County Court
- Recorders who are part-time judges sitting usually in the Crown Court though some may be assigned to the County Court
- District judges who hear small claims and other matters in the County Court
- District judges (Magistrates Court) who sit in Magistrates Courts in the major towns and cities

To become a judge at any level it is necessary to have qualified as a barrister or solicitor. It is not essential to have practiced, as the Courts and Legal Services Act 1990 provided for academic lawyers to be appointed.

Lords Justices of Appeal

Lords Justices of Appeal must have a 10-year High Court Qualification or be an existing High Court Judge.

High Court Judges

To be eligible to be a High Court Judge it is necessary either to have had the right to practice in the High Court for 10 years or more or to have been a Circuit Judge for at least 2 years. New qualifications give solicitors the chance to become High Court Judges. It is also possible for academic lawyers who have not practiced as barristers or solicitors to be appointed.

Circuit judges

To become a circuit judge a candidate can either have had rights of audience for 10 years or more in either the Crown Court or County

Court or to have been a recorder. The Courts and Legal Services Act 1990 also allows for promotion after being a district judge, stipendiary magistrate or chairman of an employment tribunal for at least three years.

Recorders

A Recorder is a part-time post. The applicant must have practiced as a barrister or solicitor for at least 10 years.

District judges

District judges need a seven year general qualification. They are appointed from either barristers or solicitors. District judges in the Magistrates Court need the same qualification.

Law Officers

There is a law office within government that advises on matters of law that affects government. There are two law officers: the Attorney General and the Solicitor General. Both are members of the government of the day and are appointed by the Prime Minister. Both will usually be Members of the House of Commons. The Attorney General appoints the Director of Public Prosecutions, who heads the Crown Prosecution Service.

The Attorney General

The Attorney General is the Government's chief legal advisor. He is not a member of the main cabinet. He will advise government on legislative proposals and on criminal proceedings which have a political or public element. He is also responsible for major litigation which involves the government. The Attorney General is appointed from those members of Parliament who are barristers and he can represent the government in court proceedings. He is the head of the English Bar but cannot practice privately as a barrister.

The Attorney General's consent is required before a prosecution can commence in certain cases such as corruption, possessing explosive substances and hijacking. He can grant immunity from prosecution and can stop proceedings for an indictable offence. He can also instruct the Director of Public Prosecutions to take over any private prosecution.

The Attorney General has the right to refer any criminal cases to the Court of Appeal (Criminal Division) for a point of law to be considered following an acquittal in the Crown Court and he can appeal against a sentence which is considered too lenient.

The Solicitor General

The Solicitor General acts as a deputy to the Attorney General.

The Director of Public Prosecutions

The DPP's duties are set out in the Prosecution of Offences Act 1985, which created the Crown Prosecution Service. The DPP must be a barrister or solicitor of at least 10 years standing. The appointment is made by the Attorney General to whom the DPP is accountable. The main function of the DPP is to head the Crown Prosecution Service. The other functions are set out in the Prosecution of Offences Act 1985, which are:

- To take over the conduct of all criminal proceedings instituted by the police
- To institute and oversee the conduct of criminal proceedings where the importance of difficulty of the proceedings makes this appropriate

- To take over the conduct of binding over proceedings brought by the police
- To give advice to police forces on all matters relating to criminal offences
- To appear for the prosecution in certain appeals

Magistrates

Lay magistrates

Lay magistrates, other wise known as Justices of the Peace sit to hear cases as a bench of two or three magistrates. Single magistrates can issue search warrants and warrants for arrest.

Lay magistrates do not have to have any qualifications in law. They must, however, be suitable in character and integrity and also have an understanding of the work that they perform. There are formal requirements as to age and residence and a magistrate must live within the area where they will sit: lay magistrates must be aged between 18 and 65 on appointment.

Some people are not eligible to be appointed, including people with a serious criminal record, though minor offences such as driving offences will not disqualify a person. Others who are disqualified are undischarged bankrupts, members of the forces and those whose work is not compatible with sitting as a magistrate, such as police officers. About 1,500 new lay magistrates are appointed each year, by the Lord Chancellor.

Duties of magistrates

Magistrates have a wide workload mainly connected to criminal cases, although they also deal with civil matters. The criminal cases involve early administrative hearings, remand hearings, bail applications and committal proceedings. They also deal with debt related civil matters such as non-payment of utility bills, council tax etc. In addition, they will also hear appeals relating to the refusal of the local authority to grant licences for the sale of alcohol and for betting and gaming establishments.

Specially trained justices will form the Youth Court to hear criminal charges against young offenders aged from 10-17years old. There is also a special panel to hear cases including orders for protection against violence, affiliation cases, adoption orders and proceedings under the Children Act 1989.

Lay magistrates also sit at the Crown Court to hear appeals from the Magistrates Court. In these cases the lay justices form a panel with a qualified judge.

The Magistrate's clerk

Every bench of magistrates is assisted by a clerk. The senior clerk in each court has to be qualified as a barrister or solicitor for at least five years. The clerk's duty is to advise the magistrates on questions of law, practice and procedure. The Crime and Disorder Act 1998 also gives clerks the powers to deal with Early Administrative Hearings.

7

Civil Cases

We have already discussed the difference between civil cases and criminal cases. Civil cases are between individuals (including companies) and criminal cases involve the state against others.

The types of disputes that can arise in civil cases are varied. The claim can be for money, from relatively small amounts to huge amounts. Contract law can be involved. An individual may be claiming compensation for injury or some other form of injustice (tort). Other types of orders sought may be for injunctions to prevent someone from doing something or the winding up of a company or divorce following a failed marriage. Civil cases are of a wide variety. In this chapter we discuss the workings of the civil courts.

Taking a case to court is expensive unless the party to a case is prepared to go down the do-it-yourself route. However, prior to going to court it is expected by the courts that some form of negotiation has taken place. Failure to do so is looked at in a dim light by any judge.

Commencing a court case in the county courts

The civil court system has undergone significant reform since the Woolf Report of 1999. Parties to a case are encouraged to give information to each other to prevent the need to go to court in the first place. This is seen as a way of ensuring that the court system does not get clogged up with unnecessary cases. Before an action is commenced and a claim is issued, a pre-action protocol should be followed. This, basically, is a list of things that should be done and if the parties to a case or potential case do not follow a procedure and give the required information to the other party, they may be liable for certain costs if they then make a court claim.

This information will usually be in the form of a letter explaining how the claim has arisen, why it is claimed that the other party is at fault, details of the injury or other damage and anything else relevant to the case. The defendant is then given three months to respond and investigate the claim admitting or denying the claim. If any other evidence is needed, such as expert evidence then the parties should agree on one expert. If this does not solve matters then it may still be necessary to go to court.

Commencing a court case

Which court?

If a decision has been made to go to court then the question will be which court? As discussed, the two courts which hear civil cases are the county court and the high court. For cases where the claim is for £15,000 or less, the case must be started in the county court. For claims larger than this amount the High court or county court can be used. There are however, some restrictions laid down as to the use of courts in the High Court and County Courts Jurisdiction Order 1991. These are that personal injury cases for less than £50,000 must be started in the county court and defamation actions must commence in the High Court.

The main consideration when commencing a claim over £15,000 is how complex the case is going to be. If it is fairly straightforward then it should commence in the county court if it is complex then the High Court should be used.

Issuing a claim against another party

If the county court is to be used, then the claim can be issued in any of the county courts in the country. If the High Court is to be used then you can go to one of the 20 District Registries or the main court in London. You will need to use a claim form called an 'N1'. The court office will supply notes on how to fill in the form. There is a fee for commencing the case and the courts will advise you of this.

Defending a claim

When a claim form is received by a defendant there are several alternatives courses of action. The defendant can admit the claim and settle. When this happens the case ends. If the claim is defended he or she may serve an acknowledgement of service (form N9) or a defence to the court within 14 days of receiving the claim. If only an acknowledgement of service is sent then the defendant has an extra 14 days to serve the defence.

If the defendant does not respond at all, the claimant can ask the court to make an order that the defendant pays the monies owed and also costs of the claim. This is called an order in default. If the case is defended then the court will allocate the case to the most suitable 'track'.

The decision on which track to be used is made by the District Judge in the county court or the Master (a procedural judge) in the High Court. The tracks are:

- The small claims track. This is normally used for disputes under £10,000, except for personal injury and housing cases where the limit is lower, usually £1,000.

- The fast track. This is normally used for straightforward disputes of £10,000-£25,000.
- The multi-track. This is for cases over £25,000 or for complex cases under this amount.

Both parties will be sent an allocation questionnaire in order to assist the judge in deciding which track to allocate the case to. Judge can also make a decision to transfer cases from one court to another.

The Small claims track

As stated, the small claims track deals with cases of £10,000 or under. People are encouraged to take their own cases so that costs are kept to a minimum. The actual process of commencing a claim is relatively simple, being paper driven. Most major towns will have a county court and addresses can be found in libraries or on the internet. These courts can hear nearly all civil cases, the main types being contract and tort cases, cases for recovery of land, disputes over partnerships, trusts and inheritance up to £30,000, divorce cases, bankruptcy, admiralty cases and matters under the Race Relations Act 1976. The county court can try small claims, fast track and multi track cases. Cases will almost always be heard in open court and members of the public are entitled to attend. The exceptions to this are matters of a more personal nature such as family matters. Cases are heard by circuit judges.

Fast-track cases

Cases of between £10,000 and £25,000 are allocated to the fast track. Personal injury cases and housing cases of between £1000 and £15,000 are also heard fast-track. Fast-track means that the court will set out a very rigid timetable for the pre-trial matters. Once a case is set down for hearing the aim is for the case to be heard within 30 weeks.

The actual trial will be heard by a circuit judge and the pre-trial hearing will last no longer than one day.

Multi-track cases

Claims for more than £25,000 are normally allocated to the multi-track. If the case was commenced in a county court then it will usually be heard there, although it can be sent to the High Court, especially if the claim is over £50,000.

The High Court

This court is based in London but has branches in 26 towns and cities throughout England and Wales. It has the power to hear any civil case and consists of three divisions each of which specialises in hearing a specific type of case: The Queens Bench Division, The Chancery Division and the Family Division.

The Queens Bench Division

The President of the Queens Bench Division is the Lord Chief Justice with up to 70 judges sitting in this division. It deals with contract and tort cases where the amount being claimed exceeds £50,000. As we have seen, a claimant can start an action for £15,000 and above. The High Court will only deal with multi-track cases. There is a right to jury in cases for fraud, libel, slander, malicious prosecution and false imprisonment cases. The role of the jury is discussed later in the book.

Commercial court

This is part of the Queens Bench division with specialist judges who will listen to commercial cases such as insurance and banking.

Admiralty court

This court deals with shipping and deciding such matters as collisions at sea and salvage rights. In 1998, the Technology and Construction

Court was set up to deal with complex building and engineering disputes.

The Queens Bench Division also has an important supervisory function over inferior courts, and other bodies with decision-making powers, such as government ministers and local councils. The process of judicial review concerns itself with whether a decision making process has been carried out legally.

The Chancery Division

The Lord Chancellor assisted by the Vice Chancellor is the head of the Chancery Division. The main business of this division involves disputes with matters such as insolvency, the enforcement of mortgages, disputes relating to trust property, copyright and patents, intellectual property and contested probate. There is also a special companies court dealing with winding up companies.

Family division

The head of the Family Division is the President and 17 High Court Judges are assigned to this division. It hears all wardship cases and all cases relating to children under the Children Act 1989. It also deals with all other family matters, such as declarations of nullity of marriage, and grants probate in non-contentious probate cases.

The Civil Procedure Rules

From 26th April 1999, new Civil Procedure Rules came into effect. Rule 1.1 of the CPR states that the overriding objective is to enable the court to deal with cases justly. Under the CPR the terminology changed to make the whole process more user friendly. For example, the word 'plaintiff' was been changed to claimant. Courts should try to:

- ensure that parties in any case are on an equal footing
- Save expense
- Deal with cases in a way which is proportionate to;
  -the amount involved (avoid costs exceeding amount claimed
  -the importance of the case
  -the complexity of the case
- Ensure that the case is dealt with quickly and fairly
- Allocate an appropriate share of the courts resources.

Judges have more control over cases than they used to, setting out timetables for cases and eliminating time wasting and actively managing cases including identifying issues at an early stage and encouraging parties to use alternative dispute resolution.

Appellate Courts

These are courts which hear appeals from lower courts. The main appellate courts are the Divisional Courts, the Court of Appeal and the Supreme Court.

Divisional Courts

Each division of the High Court has a divisional court which has the power to hear appeals from inferior courts and tribunals.

Queens Bench Divisional Court

This is the most important of the Divisional Courts and has two main functions:

1. It hears appeals by way of case stated from criminal cases decided in the Magistrates Court.
2. It has supervisory powers over inferior courts and tribunals and also over the actions and decisions of public bodies and

Government ministers. This is known as Judicial Review, as previously discussed.

The Queens Bench Divisional Court also hears matters relating to unlawful detainment and the right to liberty.

Chancery Divisional Court

The Chancery Divisional Court deals with a small number of appeals, mainly tax related appeals and appeals arising from bankruptcy cases.

Family Divisional Court

This court hears appeals from the decisions of magistrates regarding family matters and orders affecting children.

Court of Appeal (Civil Division)

The Court of Appeal has two divisions, civil and criminal. There are 35 Lord Justices of Appeal. The Civil Division is the main appellate court for civil cases and it is headed by the Master-of-the-Rolls. The Court of Appeal (Civil Division) mainly hears appeals from the following courts:

- All three divisions of the High Court
- The County Court for multi-track cases
- The Immigration Appeal Tribunal
- Some tribunals

Permission to appeal is required in most cases. It can be granted by the court where the decision was made, or by the Court of Appeal. Permission to appeal is only granted where the court feels that an appeal may have some success or there is some other reason why the appeal should be heard.

Permission to appeal is not required where the liberty of an individual is at stake.

The Supreme Court

This is the final and highest court of appeal in the English legal system. It hears appeals from the Court of Appeal, the Divisional Courts and in rare cases from the High Court.

Appeal routes in civil cases

Appeals from the County Court

The appeal routes from the County Court are set out in Part 52 of the Civil Procedure Rules. Generally:

- fast track cases dealt with by a District judge-these appeals are heard by a Circuit Judge
- For fast track cases dealt with by a circuit judge the appeal is heard by a High Court Judge
- For final decisions in multi track cases heard in the County Court the right of appeal is to the Court of Appeal

Appeals from small claims

After October 2000 appeals against decisions in small claims cases became possible. The appeal routes are the same as for fast track cases.

Appeals from the High Court

From a decision in the High Court the appeal will go to the Court of Appeal (Civil Division). In rare cases there may be a leapfrog decision to the Supreme Court.

Further appeals

From a decision of the Court of Appeal there is a further appeal to the Supreme Court but only if the Supreme Court or Court of Appeal gives its permission to appeal. If a point of European law is involved the case may be referred to the European Court of Justice. This referral can be made by an English Court.

Remedies in civil cases

The main remedy awarded by the courts is an order for financial recompense. This is termed an award of damages. The object of awarding financial damages, in contract cases, is to put the claimant in a position, as far as possible where they may have been if the breach had not occurred. This will be the same in negligence (tort) cases.

Special damages

These will be damages which can be specifically calculated. One such example may be the cost of repairing a car after a crash.

General damages

These are for areas that cannot be so readily calculated and itemised. Personal injury cases can involve pain and suffering and the amount of general damages will include the costs of future care and provision.

Nominal damages

Where a case is won but loss cannot be demonstrated the courts will be in a position to award nominal damages in recognition of an individuals rights being infringed.

Exemplary damages

These are also termed 'punitive damages'. They are damages that are intended to punish the defendant, not only compensate the claimant. Exemplary damages are not available for breach of contract and are only awarded in tort cases where they are authorised by statute, where there has been oppressive, arbitrary or unconstitutional action by servants of the government. In addition, they are awarded where the defendant intended to make a profit from the tort which would be greater than the compensation due from the tort.

Equitable remedies

The major equitable remedies are injunctions, specific performance and rescission.

Injunctions

Temporary injunctions, called interlocutory injunctions can be granted during the course of a case This is usually granted in order to preserve the status quo between then parties while the case is awaiting a full trial.

Injunctions are used in many areas of law, contract, family and employment. Breach of an injunction is a contempt of court.

Specific performance

This is a remedy only used in contract law and it is an order that a contract should only be carried out as agreed.

Rescission

This is also only available in contract cases. The aim of rescission is to return the parties to their pre-contractual position. The main ground for rescission is a misrepresentation, which caused one party to enter into a contract erroneously.

Rectification
This is a court order that a document should be altered to reflect the party's intention.

Alternative Dispute Resolution

As we have seen, using courts to solve civil cases is costly, or can be, and takes time. As a result, many people use what is knows as Alternative Dispute Resolution (ADR) in order to arrive at a solution to their problems.

In employment cases, ADR has long been used, primarily through ACAS (Advisory, Conciliation and Arbitration Service) Neutral mediators are used in some cases. However, this is only useful if there is a hope of parties to a dispute agreeing. There are a growing number of mediation services, one of the main ones being the Centre for Dispute Resolution set up in 1991.

Conciliation is similar to mediation in that there will be a third party helping to resolve the issues. Conciliators play a more active role generally than mediators.

8

Criminal Cases-Police Powers

Police Organisation

The structure of policing within the United Kingdom is complex. There are 44 geographic forces in England, Wales and Northern Ireland, each led by a Chief Constable who under statute has authority of 'direction and control' of the force. Each Chief Constable is accountable to law, to the Home Secretary for national efficiency and effectiveness, and to local democratic oversight. From November 2012, 41 of the geographic forces have elected Police and Crime Commissioners (PCCs) responsible for discharging local democratic oversight. The two exceptions are City of London Police, and the Police Service of Northern Ireland. In London, the PCC role is undertaken by the Mayor's Office for Policing and Crime (MOPAC).

As well as regionally based police forces, there is also British Transport Police with responsibility for policing the rail network, and specialist police forces such as the Ministry of Defence Police which serves MoD establishments, and the Civil Nuclear Constabulary, which protects nuclear sites.

Working alongside police officers are Community Support officers (CSO's) civilians employed by police authorities. Their powers include the ability to:

- issue fixed penalty notices for anti-social behaviour
- carry out searches and road checks
- stop and detain school truants

- deprive an individual of their liberty for up to 30 minutes until a police officer arrives, where the suspect fails to provide his name and address or it is reasonably suspected that the details provided are inaccurate.

The Serious Crime and Police Act 2005 created a national investigation agency, The Serious Organised Crime Agency (SOCA) to tackle the heads of organised crime who undertake illegal enterprises such as drug trafficking, paedophile rings and people smuggling. In June 2010, the Home Secretary announced the creation of a new National Crime Agency which will become operational in 2013.

Over time, there has been a general increase in recorded crime, with violent crime on the increase. The police are obviously in the front line dealing with crime as a whole. The main police powers are contained within the Police and Criminal Evidence Act (PACE) 1984 with amendments and additions made by the Criminal Justice and Public Order Act 1994, the Police Act 1996, the Terrorism Act 2000 and the Criminal Justice Act 2003. PACE also provides for the codes of practice giving extra details on the procedures for stop and search, detaining, questioning and identifying suspects. These are issued by the Home Secretary. PACE was significantly modified by the Serious Organised Crime and Police Act 2005 which replaced nearly all existing powers of arrest with a new general power of arrest.

Police powers

The police have to exercise their powers sensitively and respect the rights of the individual citizen. At the same time they must also have sufficient powers to enable them to do their job.

The law on police powers is mainly contained within the Police and Criminal Evidence Act 1984 and the associated codes of practice contained within section 66 of the act. There are eight codes:

- Code A deals with the powers to stop and search

- Code B for the powers to search premises and seize property
- Code C deals with detention, treatment and questioning of subjects
- Code D deals with the rules for identification procedures
- Code E deals with the tape recording of interviews with suspects
- Code F deals with visual recording of interviews
- Code G deals with statutory powers of arrest
- Code H deals with the detention of terrorism suspects

Stop and search

The powers of stop and search are primarily contained within PACE S.1-7 and code of practise A. PACE says that an officer must not stop and search unless the necessary legal power exists. Before an officer can stop a person or vehicle they must have reasonable suspicion that an individual is in possession of a prohibited article, is about to commit or has committed an arrestable offence. An officer cannot target an individuals for their age, race, appearance previous offences committed. An individual can submit to a voluntary search but the power to do so must exist in any case. An officer must give their name station and reason for the search. The officer must be of the same sex as the subject of the search and the search must take place near the location or as near as is practicable. Reasonable force may be used during the search if necessary.

A police officer can ask a person to remove their jacket, coat or gloves etc but no more. A more thorough search can take place in a private for example a police van. The officer will fill out a form explaining why they have stopped a person and should contain the details of the officer that stopped them and the outcome of the search, any prohibited items being carried may be seized.

There are exemptions to some stop and search powers under PACE where officers can stop without suspicion. These are contained in annex A of PACE amongst other these are under the Misuse of Drugs Act 1971 allowing officers stop and search for drugs, the Terrorism ACT 2000 where there is suspicion of involvement in terrorism or section 60 of the Criminal Justice and Public Order Act 1994 (CJPOA) this must be authorised by a senior officer who believes that serious violence may take place in the locality. If authorised an officer does not have to have reasonable suspicion about an individual who is stopped. Under the Crime and Disorder Act (1998) when a section 60 has been authorised an officer can ask a person to remove any item that is being used by an individual to hide their identity and they can seize that item if there is reasonable suspicion that it is being or will be used mainly for the purpose of concealing of identity. This order can last for a maximum of 24 hours unless the chief constable believes threat of violence still exists then another 24hrs may be granted.

Searching premises

The power for police to enter and search premises are mainly contained in S17 and S18 of PACE and code of practise B. This gives the police powers to enter and search premises for evidence, this can be done with or without a warrant. Premises can be searched without a warrant if the occupier gives permission to do so, permission must be given in written form, and consent can be withdrawn at any time.

If a warrant is needed the police must apply to a magistrate for it to be issued. The magistrate must believe that the police have reasonable grounds for suspecting that an indictable offence has been committed and that the premises subject to the search contain relevant and substantial evidence in relation to the investigation. It must also be impractical to gain access with the occupiers permission or that it would frustrate the aim of the search or it is know that entry would not be granted without a warrant .

The Serious and Organised Crime and Police Act 2005 introduced the powers to allow with a warrant entry to a specific premises, or any premises occupied or controlled by the person named on the warrant. It may allow for entry to the premises on more than one occasion the number of searches can be limited or unlimited these power are known together as a Super warrant. A search warrant must be used within 3 months and it must be executed at a reasonable hour. On entry to a premises the officers must identify themselves, explain why they are there, what grounds there are for the search and under what powers they do so [they need not do so upon entry if the situation would make this impracticable but they must do so before the search begins [R v Longman (1998)]. A police officer can enter and search a premises without a search warrant if it is in order to arrest a person named on an arrest warrant, to arrest someone for an arrestable offence or to recapture an escaped prisoner. An officer can also enter without a search warrant, after making an arrest if the officer believes there is evidence on the premises relating to, connected to or similar to the offence for which the person has just been arrested. An officer can enter any premises occupied or controlled by the person under arrest or any premises in which a person was in at the time of arrest or immediately before arrest. The police must make these search at the time of arrest, they may not return to search hours later [R v Badham (1987]. The police have the right to enter a premises under common law to prevent or deal with a breach of the peace. This can also apply to private dwellings. See McLeod V Commissioner of Police for the Metropolis (1994). A suspect cannot be detained without a formal arrest taking place.

Powers of arrest

The powers of arrest are contained in S.24 of Pace and code of practise G. The SOCPA replaced the old S.24 and 25 of PACE with a new section 24. Pre 2006 PACE had a definition of arrestable and non-arrestable offences. Arrestable offences being those for which a potential sentence would be in excess of 5 years and non-arrestable would be an offence for which the sentence is under 5 years. Separate definitions no longer exist since the enactment of the SOCPA. An officer can now affect an arrest for any offence as long as he believes it is necessary.

A police officer should inform a suspect as soon as possible that they are under arrest. There is no set wording that should be used so it could be enough to just say that 'you are nicked for theft'. A suspect should be cautioned on arrest. If there are grounds to suspect a person of an offence, they should be cautioned before they are questioned. A police officer can arrest without a warrant anybody who is about to commit or is committing an offence or anybody who the officer has reasonable grounds for suspecting is about to commit or is in the process of committing an offence. If a police officer has reasonable grounds to suspect an offence has been committed he may arrest anybody he has reasonable grounds to suspect is guilty of it.

If an offence has been committed an officer can arrest without warrant anybody who is guilty of the offence or anybody he has reasonable grounds to suspect is guilty of it.

To affect an arrest, an officer must believe an offence is about to be or has been committed or has reasonable grounds for suspecting an offence has happened, also it must meet the necessity criteria this means. An officer can only affect an arrest if he believes it is necessary to confirm a person's name or address if he suspects that an individual is providing false information. To prevent the person's in question; causing physical harm to themselves or others, suffering injury, causing loss of or damage to property, causing an unlawful obstruction of the highway. To protect a child or vulnerable person from harm by the person in question. To allow the prompt and effective investigation of an offence or the conduct of the person; to prevent the prosecution of an offence being hindered by the disappearance of the person or prevent a person from committing acts against public decency thought this only applies where members of the public cannot reasonably avoid the person in question.

CJPOA 1994 added powers to PACE to allow an officer to arrest without warrant anyone who has been released on police bail and has not attended the police station at the set time.

Prior to the enactment of SOCPA, PACE included a definition of non-arrestable offences. non-arrestable offences where offences that had a sentence of 5 years or less for an individual aged 21years or over. Police had powers of arrest for non-arrestable offences under S.25 of PACE, they could arrest if they believed it is necessary to confirm a person's name or address, In order to serve a summons.(if they suspected that an individual is providing false information or refuses to give details). To prevent the person's in question; causing physical harm to themselves or others, suffering injury, causing loss of or damage to property, causing an unlawful obstruction of the highway. To protect a child or vulnerable person from harm by the person in question. To allow the prompt and effective investigation of an offence or the conduct of the person; to prevent any prosecution of an offence being hindered by the disappearance of the person or prevent a person from committing acts against public decency thought this only applies where members of the public cannot reasonably avoid the person in question.

A person other than a police officer may arrest without a warrant anyone who is in the act of committing an indictable offence; anyone who he has reasonable grounds for suspecting is committing an indictable offence. If an indictable offence has been committed a person other than a police officer may arrest anyone who is guilty of the offence or anyone whom they have reasonable grounds to believe is guilty of it. These powers of arrest by non-police officers can only be exercised if they have reasonable grounds for believing that it is necessary to arrest the person in order to prevent them from causing physical harm to themselves or others; suffering physical injury;

causing loss of or damage to property or to prevent them making off before a police officer can take responsibility for them.

Once arrested a suspect must be taken to a police station as soon as is practicably possible; the police have the option of bailing the person to appear at a later date. Detainees must be informed of their rights. These include:

- Someone must/can be informed of the arrest
- Being told that independent legal advice is freely available and being allowed to consult with a solicitor
- Being allowed to consult the code of practice

Police interviews

Detained persons may be interviewed by the police. All interviews carried out at a police station must be tape recorded. Suspects have the right to a solicitor during questioning. If a solicitor is not asked for or is late questioning can commence. If the person is under 17 or is mentally handicapped there must be an 'appropriate adult' present during questioning.

Section 76 of PACE states that a court shall not allow statements which have been obtained through oppression to be used as evidence.

The right to silence

Before the mid-nineties, when suspects were being questioned by the police in relation to an offence, they had a definite right to remain silent. However, this was changed somewhat with the introduction of s.34 of the Criminal Justice and Public Order Act 1994. Although this statutory provision does not usurp this right altogether, it does set out some fundamental criteria that can be relied upon by a magistrate or jury when they may feel that a defendant should have been more cooperative at the time of the police interview. As a consequence, they can then go on to draw adverse inferences from this silence, as below:

- Not mentioning a specific fact during questioning which is later relied on in the defence

- Once charged, failure to mention a fact when it would be considered reasonable to do so

- Failing to account for marks, objects, substances or clothing that was found on the defendant at the arrest scene

- Not disclosing the reason why the defendant was at a specific place or what he or she was doing at the time of the incident

Fingerprints, DNA samples & Photographs

When you are first arrested, you can normally be fingerprinted or DNAed (*non-intimate* sample) only after you have been charged, or told that you have been reported for the offence. You cannot have an *intimate* DNA sample taken without your consent. You can also be fingerprinted or DNA'ed after you are convicted (by a court), and can be required to go to a police station for this. If you resist having fingerprints or samples taken, "reasonable force" can be used.

You can now be photographed without your consent, and force can be used (including to remove any item or substance worn on or over your head). You can always have fingerprints or samples taken if you *consent*.

Fingerprints

Fingerprints can only be taken without consent after a person has been charged, or informed that they are being 'reported'. There are two qualifications, one positive and one negative: fingerprints cannot be taken unless it's a *recordable* offence. In practice, about the only offences a person might be charged with that *aren't* recordable are 'Obstruction of the Highway' and 'Breach of the Peace'

A person can also have fingerprints taken without consent, before being charged, on the authorisation of an Inspector.

The authorisation for fingerprinting before charge can only be given if the Inspector "has reasonable grounds . . . for believing that fingerprints will tend to confirm or disprove involvement [in a criminal offence]" (PACE, s.61(4)). A copy of this authorisation should go on a person's custody record (a copy of which can be asked for after release).

In addition, a person can be required to go to a police station after they have been charged (or reported) and released, or (if convicted) after they have been convicted by a court, or after they have accepted a Caution or (if under 18) a Reprimand or Warning, in order to have fingerprints taken. This only applies if it's for a recordable offence, and if they have not had fingerprints taken before or they proved unsuitable or insufficient. They must be summoned within one month of release or conviction (or one month after the police find out that the prints are unsuitable or insufficient), and must be given at least 7 days-notice. They can be arrested without a warrant if they do not turn up. (PACE, s.63A(4)–(7))

Non-intimate DNA samples

'Non-intimate' DNA samples mean samples of hair (not pubic hair),[note] swabs taken from the mouth (but no other body orifice) or under the nail, a sample of nail, saliva or footprint etc.

The basic rule for non-intimate DNA samples is as for fingerprints: only after charge or being informed that that they will be reported (unless they consent). The qualifications to the basic rule are as follows:

- Samples cannot be taken unless it's for a *recordable* offence (see above, under fingerprints).
- A person can have a non-intimate sample taken without their consent, before being charged, on the authorisation of a Inspector.

The authorisation for taking a sample before charge can only be given if the Inspector has "reasonable grounds . . . for believing that the sample will tend to confirm or disprove involvement [in a recordable offence]" (PACE, s.63(4)). A copy of this authorisation should go on the custody record.

A person can also be required to go to a police station after they have been charged or reported and released, or after conviction, for a sample to be taken, if no sample was taken before or it proved unsuitable or insufficient. The rules are the same as for fingerprints (see above).

Intimate DNA samples

'Intimate' DNA samples mean samples of blood, semen or other tissue fluid, urine or pubic hair, dental impressions or swabs taken from a body orifice other than the mouth. These regulations are in PACE, s.62.

An intimate sample can only ever be taken (a) if a person consents (in writing), and (b) if authorised by a Superintendent. The rules for the authorisation are as for non-intimate samples (they do not have to have been charged with the offence). Note that an intimate sample can be taken from a person even after they have been released by the police, if two or more non-intimate samples have been taken already, and they have proved insufficient.

In addition, the sample must be taken by a registered doctor, registered nurse or dentist (unless it's a urine sample).

Note that, although a person cannot have an intimate sample taken without their consent, if they withhold consent without "good cause," that fact can be made known to a court, which can "draw such inferences from the refusal as appear proper.

Mandatory drugs tests

New rules are coming in regarding mandatory Class A drugs tests. Mandatory drugs testing is only available for people aged 18 or over, and in one of two situations: either, if a person has been charged with a "trigger offence," which roughly means various offences under the Theft Act 1968 or a drugs offence related to a Class A drug; or, if they have been charged with any other offence, and an Inspector has authorised the sample to be taken.

In the second case, the inspector must have "reasonable grounds for suspecting that the misuse of any specified Class A drug caused or contributed to the offence."

A person has to be asked to give the sample for the drugs test, which can be either a non-intimate sample or a urine sample. But it is a specific offence to refuse to give the sample "without good cause." The sample can be used by a court in sentencing after conviction, and also in deciding whether to grant bail.

National fingerprint and DNA databases

In every case when fingerprints or DNA samples are taken at a police station, they can be the subject of a "speculative search" in the national databases. A person should be informed about this by the police when the prints or samples are taken. (PACE, s.63A(1))

Fingerprints and samples **no longer** have to be destroyed once a person is acquitted, or if the case against them is dropped, but in those cases they can only be used for the purposes of investigation of crime. They also do not have to be destroyed if a person accepts a Caution for the offence. (PACE, s.64(1)–(3), as amended by the Criminal Justice and Police Act 2001).

Complaints against the police

People who believe that the police have acted unjustly and exceeded their powers can complain and the type of complaint will determine how it is dealt with. Minor complaints are dealt with informally and more serious complaints will be dealt with at a higher level.

The Independent Police Complaints Commission

This was set up in 2004 to supervise the handling of complaints against the police and associated staff, such as Community Support Officers. The IPCC sets down standards for the police to follow when dealing with complaints. They also monitor the way complaints are dealt with by local police forces.

The IPCC will also investigate serious issues including any accident involving death or serious injury, allegations of corruption, allegations against senior officers, allegations involving racism and allegations of perverting the course of justice.

Any member of the public can complain and complaints can be made directly to the IPCC or through organisations such as the Citizens Advice Bureau or through the Equality and Human Rights Commission or the Youth Offending Team. It is also possible to complain through a solicitor or an MP. Where the police have committed a crime in the execution of their duties criminal action can be brought against them.

9

Hearing Criminal Cases

As the criminal law is set down by the state, bringing a prosecution for breach of criminal law is seen as the role of the state. The majority of prosecutions are brought by the Crown Prosecution Service which is the agency of the state for criminal prosecutions.

A criminal prosecution can also be brought by an individual or company although this is rare. The following is an outline of the procedure for criminal trials.

Pre-trial hearings

All criminal cases will first go to the magistrates court and, in most cases, will be referred to a higher court unless the offence is minor or the person(s) plead guilty.

Categories of criminal offences

Criminal offences are divided into three main categories as follows:

1. Summary offences. These are the least serious and are always tried in the Magistrates Court. They include nearly all driving offences, common assault and criminal damage of less than £5,000.
2. Triable either way offences. These are a middle range type offence and can include assault causing actual bodily harm. These cases can be tried either in the Magistrates Court or the Crown Court.

3. Indictable offences. These are more serious crimes such as rape or murder. All such offences must be tried at the Crown Court, the first hearing being at the Magistrates Court.

Bail

One matter to be decided pre-trial is that of bail, whether the defendant should stay in custody while awaiting trial or whether he or she should be released on bail. Being granted bail means that the person is at liberty until the next stage of the case.

The police may release a suspect on bail while they pursue their enquiries. The suspect must return to the police station at a specified date in the future. The police can also grant bail to a defendant who has been charged with an offence. In this case the person is bailed to appear at a Magistrates Court at a later date. The decision on whether to grant bail or not is made by a custody officer under section 38 of PACE. Bail can be refused if the suspects name and address cannot be ascertained or there is doubt as to the validity of information.

The principles as to when bail should be granted are contained within the Bail Act 1976. This is the key Act, starting with the assumption that an accused person should be granted bail, though this right can be limited for certain cases such as terrorism or repeat serious offences. Section 4 of the Bail Act 1976 gives a general right to bail, but this can be withdrawn if the court believes that there are grounds for believing the defendant, if released, would fail to surrender to custody, commit an offence whilst on bail or interfere with witnesses or obstruct the course of justice.

In deciding whether to grant bail the court will consider various factors:
*   The nature and seriousness of the offence
*   The character of the defendant and community ties
*   The record of the defendant
*   The strength of evidence against the defendant.

The courts have the powers to impose conditions on the granting of bail. These are similar to those granted to the police, as outlined below.

Bail sureties

The courts or police can require a surety for bail. This is another person who is willing to pay a sum of money if that person doesn't turn up to court. No money is paid until the defendant breaks bail.

If any person granted bail by the police fails to attend the next stage of the case then the police can make an arrest.

Like the courts, the police have powers to impose conditions on bail. These are contained within the Criminal Justice and Public Order Act 1994. These conditions can vary, ranging from surrender of passport to regular reporting at a police station.

If the police are not prepared to grant bail then they must bring the suspect before a magistrate's court. The magistrates can then make a decision as to whether the suspect should be released on bail.

Restrictions on bail do exist, such as terrorism cases and situations where there have been repeated serious offences.

Section 19 of the Criminal Justice Act 2003 amended the Bail Act 1976 and placed certain restrictions on bail for adult drug offenders who have tested positive for specific Class A drugs where the offender is either charged with possession or possession with intent to supply a Class A drug or the court is satisfied that there are grounds for believing that misuse of a class A drug contributed to the offence or that the offence was motivated wholly or partly by the intended misuse of a drug and the defendant has refused to participate in an assessment or follow up in relation to the dependency on Class A drugs.

The prosecution in a case can appeal against the granting of bail. This is set out in the Bail (Amendment) Act 1993.

The Crown Prosecution Service

The CPS was created by the Prosecution of Offences Act 1985 and is headed by the Director of Public Prosecutions. The Director operates under the superintendence of the Attorney General, who is accountable to Parliament for the Service. The Director is supported by a Chief Executive, who is responsible for running the business on a day-to-day basis, allowing the Director to concentrate on prosecution, legal issues and criminal justice policy.

The CPS is divided into 13 geographical Areas across England and Wales. Each Area is led by a Chief Crown Prosecutor (CCP) who is responsible for the provision of a high quality prosecution service in their Area. Each CCP is supported by an Area Business Manager (ABM), and their respective roles mirror, at a local level, the responsibilities of the DPP and Chief Executive. Administrative support to Areas is provided by Area Operations Centres. A 'virtual' 14th Area, CPS Direct, is also headed by a CCP and provides out-of-hours charging decisions to the police.

Two specialist casework groups - Central Fraud Group and Serious Crime Group - deal with the prosecution of all cases investigated by the Serious & Organised Crime Agency, UK Borders Agency and Her Majesty's Revenue & Customs as well as serious crime, terrorism, fraud and other challenging cases that require specialist experience.

The CPS is effectively the largest law firm in the UK, dealing exclusively with criminal cases and casework issues arising from them. At the end of March 2013, it employed a total of 6,841 people. About 34% are qualified prosecutors and 93% of all staff are engaged in, or support, frontline prosecutions. The functions of the CPS involve all aspects of prosecution as outlined below:

- Deciding on what offences should be charged
- Reviewing all cases given to them by the police to see if there is sufficient evidence to proceed and whether it is in the public interest to do so
- Taking responsibility for the case
- Conducting the prosecution of cases in the Magistrates Court
- Conducting cases in the Crown Court

Once a defendant has been charged with an offence then the police role in the matter is over and the case is handed over to the CPS.

Criminal courts

The two courts which hear criminal cases are the Magistrates Court and the Crown Court. If a defendant in either one of these courts pleads guilty to a charge against them the role of the court is to pass sentence. Where the accused pleads not guilty the role of the court is to try the case and establish whether the defendant is guilty or not guilty. The burden of proof is on the prosecution who must prove the case beyond reasonable doubt. The form of trial is adversarial with prosecution and defence presenting their cases and cross-examining witnesses while the role of the judge is to be a referee, overseeing the trial and ensuring that the law is adhered to. The judge does not investigate the case.

The role of the Magistrates Court

There were about 430 Magistrates Courts in England and Wales. However, this has now been significantly reduced following a review of the court estate began in 2010. Magistrates Courts are local courts and they will be in almost every town whilst big cities will usually have several. Cases are heard by magistrates, who may be either qualified District Judges or unqualified lay justices. There is a legally qualified clerk attached to each court to provide assistance.

Magistrates Courts have jurisdiction in a variety of matters. They will:

- Try all summary cases
- Try any triable either way offences which it has been decided should be dealt with in the Magistrates Court
- Deal with the first hearings of all indictable offences
- Deal with other matters connected to criminal offences such as issuing warrants for bail and deciding bail applications
- Try cases in the Youth Court where the defendant is aged 10-17

The Magistrates Courts also have some civil jurisdiction including enforcing council tax demands and issuing warrants of entry and investigation to utilities such as gas and electricity, family cases, proceedings concerning the welfare of children under the Children Act 1989.

Summary Trials

Summary trials are the least serious criminal offences. They are further divided into offences on different levels ranging from level one (lowest) to level five (highest). Fines are set in accordance with each level. For level one the fine is maximum £200, level two £500, level three £1,000, level four £2,500 and level five £5,000. These fines arise from the Criminal Justice Act 1991 and are increased periodically to account for inflation. The maximum prison sentence that can be given for summary offences is six months which will shortly be increased to 15 months following the passing of the Criminal Justice Act 2003.

At the start of any summary trial the defendant will be asked whether he or she pleads guilty or not guilty. If a guilty plea is entered the case will be explained to the court and the prosecutor and defence will put their case and the magistrates will decide sentence.

If a not guilty plea is entered, the procedure is rather more complicated as the prosecutor has to provide evidence to the court and prove the case. Witnesses are called. At the end the defence can call for the case to be dismissed on lack of evidence if this is the case. The magistrates will then decide on the case, whether guilty or not guilty.

Triable either way cases

Plea before venue

Under this procedure the defendant is asked whether he pleads guilty. If the plea is guilty then there is no right to ask to go to a Crown Court although the magistrate may still decide to send him there for sentence.

If the defendant pleads not guilty then the magistrates must carry out 'mode of trial' proceedings to establish where the case will be tried. Under section 19 of the Magistrates Court Act 1980 they must consider the nature and seriousness of the case and decide a course of action. If the case involves complex cases of law it will usually be referred to the Crown Court. It will also be referred to the Crown Court if it is of a particularly serious nature and has, for example, involved organised crime or where the amount involved was particularly high, more than twice the potential fine that magistrates can levy.

In cases, rare cases, where the Attorney General, Solicitor General or Director of Public Prosecutions is the prosecutor, magistrates must abide by the wishes of the prosecutor and send the case to the Crown Court if this is what is wanted.

If magistrates accept jurisdiction, the defendant is informed that he has the right to trial by jury, in the Crown Court, but may be tried by magistrates if he so wishes. If the magistrates feel that they have insufficient powers to punish they can refer the matter to the Crown Court for sentencing.

Sending cases to the Crown Court

For indictable offences the case is automatically referred by magistrates to the Crown Court. Section 51 of the Crime and Disorder Act 1988 dictates this. For triable either way offences, magistrates will hold a plea before venue and, if the plea is not guilty, a mode of trial hearing. The decision to try the case in the Magistrates Court or the Crown Court is taken at this point.

Committal proceedings

Magistrates can commit a defendant charged with a triable either way offence for sentence in the Crown Court.

Role of the court clerk

Every bench of magistrates is assisted by a clerk who is also a legal advisor. The senior clerk in each court has to be a barrister or solicitor of at least five years standing. The role of the clerk is to guide the magistrates on questions of law, practice and procedure.

Youth courts

Youth offenders aged between 10-17 are dealt with in the Youth court which is a branch of the Magistrates court. Children under the age of 10 cannot be charged with a criminal offence. There are some exceptional cases where the case can be tried in the Crown Court if the charge is one of manslaughter or murder, rape or causing death by dangerous driving. In addition, it is possible to send a person over 14 to the Crown Court if the charge is sufficiently serious.

Appeals from the Magistrates Court

The system of appeal routes from the magistrate's court will depend on whether the appeal is on a point of law or for other reasons. The two appeal routes are the Crown Court or the Queens Bench Divisional Court.

The normal route of appeal is the Crown Court and can only be used by the defence. If the defendant has pleaded guilty then the appeal can only be against sentence. If the plea was not guilty then the appeal can be against conviction or sentence. In both cases the defendant has the automatic right to appeal.

Further appeal to the Supreme Court

From the decision of the Queens Bench Court there is a possibility of a further appeal to the Supreme Court. This can only be made if:

1. The Divisional Court certifies that a point of law of general public importance is involved.
2. The Divisional Court or the Supreme Court gives leave to appeal because the point is one which ought to be considered by the Supreme Court.

The Crown Court

The Courts Act 1971 set up the Crown Court to deal with all cases that were not tried at the Magistrates Court. The Crown Court sits in 90 different centres throughout England and Wales. There are three kinds of centre:

1. First tier-these exist in main centres throughout the country. At each court there is a High court and a Crown Court. The Crown Court is staffed by High Court Judges as well as Circuit Judges and Recorders. The court can deal with all categories of crime triable on indictment.
2. Second tier-this is a Crown Court only, but High Court judges can sit there on a regular basis to hear cases, as well as Circuit Judges and Recorders.

3. Third tier-this is staffed by Circuit judges and Recorders. The most serious cases are not usually tried here.

Preliminary matters in the Crown Court

The indictment

The indictment is a document which formally sets out charges against a defendant.

Disclosure by prosecution and defence

The Criminal Procedure and Investigations Act 1996 places a duty on both sides to make certain points of the case known to each other. The 1996 Act also imposes a duty on the defence in cases which are to be tried on indictment. After the prosecutors initial disclosure, the defence must give a written statement to the prosecution setting out:

1. the nature of the accused persons defence
2. the matters on which he takes issue with the prosecution and why he intends to take issue
3. any point of law which he wishes to take, and the case authority on which he will rely.
4.

Details of alibis and witnesses he intends to call to support the alibi. This information gives the prosecution time to carry out police checks on the witnesses.

A preliminary hearing called a 'plea and directions' hearing is held after a case has been forwarded to a Crown Court, normally within four weeks if the defendant is being held in custody and six weeks if not. The purpose of this hearing is to discover whether the plea is guilty or not guilty. All charges are read out in open court and the defendant will plead one way or the other. This is called the 'arraignment'. If the defendant pleads guilty the judge will sentence the defendant immediately, if possible. Where a defendant pleads not guilty the judge will require the defence and prosecution to identify the key issues of fact and law that are involved in the case. He will then give directions that are necessary for the organisation of the trial.

The trial

A defendant appearing at the Crown Court will usually be represented by a barrister and sometimes a solicitor. Defendants can represent themselves and can, in most cases, cross-examine witnesses although there are some cases where this cannot happen, such as sexual offences.

The order of events at a trial will depend on whether the defendant pleads guilty or not guilty. If the plea is not guilty the following will happen:

- The jury is sworn in to try the case
- The prosecution will make an opening speech outlining the case to the jury
- The prosecution witnesses give evidence and can be cross examined by the defence-other evidence can be produced
- At the end of the prosecutions presentation the defence can state that there is no case to go to the jury: if the judge decides that this is so then he will direct the jury to acquit the defendant
- The defence may make an opening speech provided that they intend calling evidence other than the defendant
- The defence witnesses give evidence and are cross examined by the prosecution
- The prosecutor makes a closing speech pointing out the strengths of the case to the jury
- The defence makes a closing speech pointing out the weaknesses of the case

- The judge sums up the case to the jury and directs them on any law relevant to the case
- The jury retire to consider their verdict
- The jury returns and gives their verdict
- If the verdict is guilty the judge then sentences the accused, if not guilty the defendant is discharged.

It is normal, once acquitted, that the defendant cannot be re-tried. However, Under the Criminal Justice Act 2003 the double jeopardy rule was removed for serious cases if new and compelling evidence comes to light.

Appeals in criminal cases

The defendant can appeal against conviction to the Court of Appeal (Criminal Division). The appeal must be lodged verbally at the court or within 14 days of the sentence in writing. A notice of appeal must be lodged with the Court of Appeal within 28 days.

The Criminal Appeal Act 1995 states that the Court of Appeal:

a) shall allow an appeal against conviction if they think that the conviction is unsafe; and
b) shall dismiss such an appeal in any other case.

The Court of Appeal can allow an appeal and quash the conviction, vary the sentence or overturn the appeal. A re-trial can also be ordered with a new jury. The prosecution also has limited rights of appeal. In the case of jury tampering an appeal against a not guilty finding is allowed. In addition, under s 36 of the Criminal Justice Act 1972 the Attorney General can refer a point of law to the Court of Appeal. The decision does not affect the acquittal but can influence future law. Under s36 of the Criminal Justice Act 1988 the Attorney general can apply for leave to refer what is considered to be an unduly lenient sentence to the Court of Appeal for re-sentencing.

Appeals to the Supreme Court

Both prosecution and defence may appeal from the Court of Appeal to the Supreme Court. However, it is necessary to get the case certified as involving a point of law of general public importance, either from the Court of appeal or the House of Lords.

References to the European Court of Justice

In a case where a point of European law is involved it is possible for any court to make reference to the European Court of Justice under Article 177 of the Treaty of Rome.

Sentencing

Judges and magistrates have a fairly wide discretion when it comes to passing sentence on a guilty party, although they are subject to certain restrictions. Magistrates can only impose a maximum of six months imprisonment for one offence and twelve months for two. The Criminal Justice Act 2003 provides powers to increase the sentence for one offence to 12 months and two or more offences 15 months.

Judges in the Crown Court can impose up to life imprisonment for some crimes and there is no maximum figure for fines.

There are certain other restrictions placed on the Magistrates and Crown Courts by Parliament. The maximum sentence to be handed out varies depending on the crime and Parliament determines the length of sentences.

Murder carries a mandatory life sentence, whereas the judge can work within the parameters of maximum of life for other crimes such as rape and manslaughter.

When judges or magistrates pass sentence they will look at what they are trying to achieve when sentencing. Section 142 of the Criminal Justice Act 2003 sets out the purpose of sentencing for those aged 18 and over. This states that the court must have regard to:

- the punishment of offenders
- the reduction of crime
- the reform and rehabilitation of offenders
- the protection of the public
- the making of reparation by offenders to persons affected by their offences

Courts have several different types of sentences available to them. There are four main categories: custodial sentences, community sentences, fines and discharges.

Custodial sentences

This is imprisonment and is the most serious sentence that a court can pass. Prison can range from a weekend to life. Custodial sentences include:

- mandatory and discretionary life sentences
- fixed term sentences
- short term sentences
- intermittent custody
- suspended sentences

Community sentences

Prior to the Criminal Justice Act 2003, the courts had individual community sentences that they could impose on an offender. The Act created one community order under which the courts can combine any requirements that they think are necessary. These requirements include all the previous existing community sentences which become available as 'requirements' or sentences required to rehabilitate the offender, and can be attached to the sentence. The sentence is available for offenders of 16 or over. The full list of 'requirements' is set out in s 177 of the Criminal Justice Act 2003 which states:

'177 (1) Where a person aged 16 or over is convicted of an offence, the court by or before which he is convicted may make an order imposing on him any one or more of the following requirements:

a) an unpaid work requirement
b) an activity requirement
c) a programme requirement
d) a prohibited activity requirement
e) a curfew requirement
f) an exclusion requirement
g) a residence requirement
h) a mental health treatment requirement
i) a drug rehabilitation requirement
j) an alcohol treatment requirement
k) a supervision requirement
l) in the case where an offender is under 25, an attendance centre requirement.

Fines

The maximum fine in a Magistrates court is £5,000. The magistrates can impose a fine of up to £20,000 on businesses which have committed offences under various regulatory legislation such as health and safety at work.

Discharges

A discharge can be conditional or absolute. Conditional discharge means that the discharge is on condition that no further offence is committed in a set period up to three years. An absolute discharge means that no penalty has been imposed.

Other powers available to the courts

Courts can order compensation to a victim of crime. In the Magistrates court the maximum compensation is £5,000. If the defendant still has the property that he took from the victim then the court can order that it be returned. This is called a restitution order.

A court can order that a person be deprived of property that he has used to commit the offence. There is special power to order forfeiture in drug related cases. The Proceeds of Crime Act 1995 also gives the courts powers to take from criminals all profits from crime for up to six years before conviction.

Young offenders

As with adult offenders the courts have powers to order custodial sentences, fines and discharges but there are a range of different sentences available and also restrictions on what the courts can order. As far as community sentences are concerned, young offenders aged 16 or over can be given the same sentences as adults. They cannot be used for offenders under the age of 16. However, Curfew Orders can be used for those over 10 years of age. There are a number of other orders aimed at young offenders:

Attendance centre orders

This type of order is only for those under 25 and is available for all young offenders from 10 years onwards. It involves attendance at a special centre for two or three hours a week up to a maximum of 36 hours for 16-24 year olds and 24 hours for 10-15 year olds. The minimum number of hours is usually 12 but can be less for offenders under 14. The centres are run by the probation services and are usually on a Saturday afternoons. An attendance centre order cannot be made if an offender has served a period of detention previously.

Supervision orders

Section 69 of the Crime and Disorder Act 1998 created a new community order called an Action Plan order. The courts can impose this on offenders under the age of 18. The order places the offender under supervision and also sets out requirements the offender has to comply with in respect to his actions and whereabouts during a period of three months. The requirements can be any one of the following:

- To participate in set activities
- To present himself to a specified person at set times and places
- To attend at an attendance centre
- To stay away from certain places
- To comply with arrangements for his education
- To make reparation

Fines for young offenders

The maximum amount of the fine varies with the age of the offender. 10-13 year olds can only be fined a maximum of £250, 14-17 year olds £1,000. Those over 18 are subject to adult rules.

Reparation orders

A Reparation Order may be imposed on offenders under the age of 18. This order cannot be made in combination with a custodial sentence. Community Service Order, a combination order, a Supervision Order or an Action Plan Order.

An order will require the defendant to make reparation as defined in the order:

- To a person or persons who were victims of the offence or were otherwise affected by it, or
- To the community at large

The order is for a maximum of 24 hours work and the order must be completed under supervision within three months of its imposition. An order for direct reparation to a person can only be made with that persons consent.

Discharges

These may be used for an offender of any age and are most commonly used for young first time offenders who have committed minor crimes. The courts cannot conditionally discharge an offender where a child or young offender has been warned within the previous two years, unless there are exceptional circumstances. Also, the courts cannot conditionally discharge an offender where the offender is in breach of an anti-social behaviour order or where the offender is in breach of a sex offender order.

Reprimands and warnings

These are methods with which the police can deal with young offenders without bringing them to court. There is a limit to the number of times and occasions that an offender can be cautioned.

Responsibility of parents

Parents can be bound over to keep their child under control for a set period of time up to one year. The parents must agree to this. If the child then commits an offence within this period the parents must pay a sum up to £1,000 maximum.

Where an offender under 16 is fined or ordered to pay compensation, the court must order the parents to pay. The financial situation of the parents is taken into account when assessing the amount.

Parenting orders

Parenting orders are intended to offer training and support to parents to help change their children's offending behaviour. Under a parenting order a parent can be required to attend counselling or guidance sessions for up to three months on a basis of a maximum once per week.

In addition, the parent may be required to comply with conditions imposed by the court. A court may make a parenting order where:

- The court makes a Child safety Order
- The court makes an anti-social behaviour order or sex offender order in respect of the child
- A child or young person is convicted of an offence
- A parent is convicted of an offence related to truancy under the Education Act 1996.

Offenders who are mentally ill

The law recognises, as far as it possibly can, that mentally ill offenders should receive treatment as opposed to punishment. Courts have a wide range of powers available to them when dealing with such offenders. The main extra powers available to courts are to give the offender a community sentence with a requirement that he or she attends for treatment, make a hospital order or to make a restriction order under the Mental Health Act 1983 section 41.

Under the same section, offenders with severe mental health problems can be sent to high security hospitals such as Broadmoor. Such an order can only be made by the Crown Court.

Anti-social behaviour orders

Known as ASBO's these are civil orders. They are imposed on a person who has behaved in an anti-social way. The type of behaviour termed anti-social is very wide and can include drunkenness, drug taking or causing prolonged and excessive nuisance to neighbours or the wider community.

Under an ASBO a person can be ordered not to repeat a certain anti-social behaviour or not to go to a certain place. In short it has the effect of an injunction.

There is currently a wide ranging review of Anti-Social behaviour orders following the election of the coalition government in 2011. this is because it is seen that ASBO's are largely ineffective and don't achieve their main purpose.

10

Juries

Juries have been in the legal system for a long time, over one thousand years. Only a small percentage of cases is tried by jury today. However, juries are used in the following courts:

- Crown Court for criminal trials on indictment
- High Court (Queens Bench Division (only for certain cases)
- County Court for similar cases to the Queens Bench Division
- Coroners Courts

The most important use of juries is in the Crown Court in criminal trials, where they decide the guilt or otherwise of the defendant. However, given that most criminal cases are decided in the Magistrates Court only about 1% of all criminal cases are tried in the Crown Court by jury.

Civil cases

Juries in civil cases are used in only limited circumstances. The present rules for when juries may be tried in civil cases are set out in section 69 of the Supreme Court Act 1981 for High Court cases, and section 66 of the County Courts Act 1984 for cases in the County Court. The Acts state that parties have the right to jury trial only in the following types of case:

- Defamation
- False imprisonment
- Malicious prosecution
- Fraud

The present qualifications to be a juror are set out in the Juries Act 1974 (as amended). To qualify for jury service a person must be:

- Aged between 18-70
- Registered as a voter
- Resident in the United Kingdom, the Channel Islands or the Isle of man for at least five years since their thirteenth birthday and must not be:
- A mentally disordered person or disqualified from jury service

Disqualification from jury service involves having a criminal record, usually one that has entailed serving a term in prison, a suspended sentence or a community sentence. In addition, anyone who is currently on bail in criminal proceedings is disqualified from sitting as a juror.

Selecting a jury

At each Crown Court there is an official who is responsible for summonsing enough jurors to try the cases to be heard in each two-week period. The official will arrange for names to be selected at random from the electoral registers for the area which the court covers. Those summonsed must notify the court of for any reason they cannot attend. All others are expected to attend for two weeks jury service. If a trial carries on for longer than two weeks then the jury will be expected to stay on longer.

Routine police checks are carried out on prospective jurors to eliminate those with unsuitable criminal backgrounds. A further check is made on a juror's background to ascertain political affiliations although this should be carried out only in exceptional circumstances and can only be carried out with the Attorney General's permission.

Juries are usually divided into groups of 15 and 12 will be selected to hear a case. Once they have been selected these jurors come into the jury box to be sworn in as jurors. At this point, before the jury has been sworn in, both the prosecution and defence have certain rights to challenge one or more of the jurors. There are two challenges that can be made and, in addition, the prosecution have a special right of 'stand by'. These are:

- to the array
- for cause
- prosecution right to stand by jurors

To the array-this right to challenge arises from the Juries Act 1974 and it is a challenge to the whole jury on the basis that it has been chosen in an unrepresentative or biased way.

For causes-this involves challenging the right of an individual juror to sit on a jury.

Prosecution right to stand by jurors-this is a right that only the prosecution can exercise. It allows the juror who has been stood by to be put at the end of the list of potential jurors so that they will not be used unless there is a lack of jurors.

Juries role in criminal cases

The jury is only used at the Crown Court where the defendant pleads not guilty. The trial is presided over by a judge and the functions split between judge and jury. The judge will decide points of law and the jury decides the facts. At the end of a case, the judge can direct a jury to acquit a defendant if he feels that the prosecutions evidence does not make a case. This is called a directed acquittal.

Majority verdicts

If, after at least two hours (longer where there are several defendants) the jury have not reached a verdict the judge can call them back into the courtroom and direct them to pass a majority verdict. Where there is a full jury of 12, the verdict can be 10-2 or 11-1 either for guilty or not guilty. If the jury has fallen below 12 for any reason then only one can disagree with the verdict. A jury cannot go below nine.

The jury discussion takes place in secret and there can be no enquiry as to how the jury reached its verdict. Section 8 of the Contempt of Court Act 1981 makes disclosure of anything that happens in a jury room a contempt of court which is a criminal act.

11

Legal Aid and Advice

Many people will require legal assistance of one sort or another when either taking or defending a legal action. Lack of knowledge and difficulty in meeting costs are the two main reasons for needing assistance.

One principal issue for the provision of legal services (both civil and criminal) is the quantum of public funding-as the Justice Secretary explained on 30th June 2010:

'Our legal aid system has grown to an extent that we spend more than almost anywhere else in the world. France spends £3 per head of the population, Germany £5, New Zealand £8. In England and Wales, we spend a staggering £38 per head of population.

Anther principal issue is the nature of services provided (advice, professional, representation or both) in respect of criminal and civil law.

See below for changes to the system of legal aid.

The Access to Justice Act 1999 created the Legal Services Commission and replaced the old legal aid schemes with the Community Legal service for civil matters and the Criminal Defence Service for criminal cases.

To oversee the public funding of legal services the Legal Services Commission was created.

The Legal Services Commission

Section 1 of the Access to Justice Act 1999 set up this Commission. The members are appointed by the Lord Chancellor. The Legal Services Commission took over funding of civil cases from the Legal Aid Board. It is responsible for managing the Community Legal Service Fund and is responsible for developing plans locally and nationally for legal funding.

The Community Legal Service

The CLS provides the following services for matters involving civil law:
- General information about the law and legal system and availability of legal services
- Help in preventing or settling or otherwise resolving disputes about legal rights and duties
- Help in enforcing decisions by which such disputes are resolved
- Help in relation to legal proceedings not related to disputes

This scheme includes advice, assistance and representation by lawyers as well as the services of non-lawyers. It also covers mediation. The money to fund this comes from the Community Legal Services fund.

Legal aid generally

In an effort to cut the £2bn annual legal aid bill in England and Wales by £350m a year, there are soon to be fewer types of civil proceedings for which people can get funding, while changes to funding for criminal cases also looks set to change.

What is changing?

The government says it is targeting resources at those most in need with the changes in the Legal Aid, Sentencing and Punishment of

Offenders Act, which comes into force from April 2013. It reverses the position where legal aid has been available for all civil cases except those specifically excluded by the Access to Justice Act 1999. The new act removes some types of case from the scope of legal aid funding, and says other cases will only qualify when they meet certain criteria.

Which cases no longer qualify?

The government is removing funding from entire areas of civil law. They include:

- Private family law, such as divorce and custody battles
- Personal injury and some clinical negligence cases
- Some employment and education law
- Immigration where the person is not detained
- Some debt, housing and benefit issues

What cases will continue to be funded?

They include:

- Family law cases involving domestic violence, forced marriage or child abduction
- Mental health cases
- All asylum cases
- Debt and housing matters where someone's home is at immediate risk

What options are available to people ineligible for legal aid?

Many people will have to pay privately for advice or use no-win, no-fee lawyers, seek support from one of a number of charities that offer legal help, or represent themselves in trying to solve their disputes.

Opposition to the changes

The parliamentary passage of the bill saw it defeated 14 times in the House of Lords, and ultimately passed by the narrowest of margins - a tied vote which means a government victory.

There are concerns that the changes will deny justice to the poorest in society. Labour's shadow justice minister Lord Bach said the justice system was based on "equality of law", and the new restrictions were "absolutely scandalous" for "attacking... the very poorest and the most disadvantaged".

President of the Supreme Court, Lord Neuberger, warned that people who felt they were being denied access to justice could end up "taking the law into their own hands". The changes could also end up costing the government more, he suggested, as increasing numbers of people representing themselves might "mean that court hearings will last longer, the burden on court staff and judges will increase".

Government response

The Ministry of Justice says it considers legal aid an "essential part of the justice system, but can never lose sight of the fact it is paid for by taxpayers and resources are not limitless".

Other costs being cut

At present, anyone with assets worth less than £8,000 qualifies for legal aid - with those worth up to £3,000 paying nothing and others expected to make a contribution. There will also be a 10% cut in fees paid in civil and family cases.

Legal aid for criminal cases

Criminal defence makes up more than half of legal aid expenditure.

The government has previously announced measures to strengthen the Crown Court means-testing scheme, including the seizure of assets of convicted criminals to recoup the cost of a failed defence. This step can be taken from July 2013. Also this year, the government is consulting on proposed further changes, including the possibility of introducing price competition in the criminal legal aid market.

Providers of services

Legal services are provided by a broad range of people and organisations. Local solicitors are a main provider but there are other agencies such as advice agencies and consumer protection groups who can provide advice.

The Legal Services Commission grants contracts to service providers. There are currently about 5,000 firms of solicitors with contracts and they have to meet stringent criteria based on quality of advice given. However, in keeping with the other wide-ranging changes the number of contracts awarded will be restricted in the future.

Conditional fees and damage-based agreements

There are two types of no win no fee cases: conditional fee agreements (CFAs) and damages-based agreements (DBAs, sometimes called contingency fees). For both types of no win no fee cases, the lawyer's payment is conditional on the case being successful. If the case is lost, the lawyer is not paid. If the case is won, the lawyer is paid: the normal fee plus an uplift or success fee (CFAs); or a percentage of the damages recovered (DBAs).

Conditional fee agreements (CFAs)

CFAs have been used in civil litigation since the 1990s. CFAs are a means of funding litigation, usually entered into by claimants, where the lawyer agrees not to take a fee if the claim fails. If the claim is successful, the lawyer will charge an uplift (known as a success fee) in addition to his base costs. They have been particularly used in damages cases, such as for personal injury.

The previous arrangements meant that the winning party's 'success fee' is payable by the losing party in addition to the ordinary legal costs of the winning party. This adds substantially to costs for defendants. From 1 April 2013, the 'success fee' is no longer payable by the losing side; if one is charged it will be paid by the winning party, typically out of damages recovered. The 'success fee' can be up to 100% of basic fee – this remains unchanged from when CFAs were first introduced in the 1990s. However, in personal injury cases, the success fee that the lawyer may charge must not exceed 25% of the damages, excluding damages for future care and loss. This is designed to protect claimants' damages in personal injury cases, and will ensure that any damages for future care and loss are protected in their entirety.

Damages-based agreements (DBAs)

DBAs are a means of funding cases. Under a DBA, lawyers are not paid if they lose a case but may take a percentage of the damages recovered for their client as their fee if the case is successful. Before 1 April 2013, DBAs could not be used in civil litigation. However, they could be used in other areas, for example in tribunals such as the employment tribunal. The Damages-Based Agreements Regulations 2010 regulated the use of DBAs in employment tribunals until 1 April 2013, when they were superseded by the Damages-Based Agreements Regulations 2013.

From 1 April 2013, DBAs can be used in civil litigation and new regulations have been made, incorporating the earlier provisions in respect of employment tribunals.

There are different requirements in the regulations as between civil litigation and employment tribunal cases, as civil litigation can only be conducted by authorised lawyers, who act under professional rules of conduct. Employment tribunal matters can be conducted by others, including claims managers, who do not have professional rules of conduct, and additional safeguards are therefore provided in the regulations.

The maximum payment that the lawyer can recover from the claimant's damages is capped – at 25% of damages (excluding damages for future care and loss) in personal injury cases; at 35% of damages on employment tribunal cases (which has existed since 2010); and at 50% of damages in all other cases.

Successful claimants using DBAs will recover their costs (the lawyer's hourly rate fee and disbursements) from defendants in the usual way, but the claimant will be responsible for paying from their damages any shortfall between the solicitors' costs paid by the losing defendant and the agreed DBA fee and will also be required to pay any shortfall in respect of disbursements. Lawyers acting under a DBA will be required to comply with the indemnity principle, which means that their fee would be restricted to what is due under the DBA fee: if the DBA fee is less than the solicitors' costs would be in the absence of a DBA, a losing defendant would only be liable to pay the DBA fee.

Law centres

Law centres offer a free non-means tested legal service to people in their area. Funding has always been a problem for law centres and many are reliant on grants. As a result many have closed. Those which have remained open will deal with the needs of the community they serve, undertaking work such as housing, planning, the environment, employment, immigration and consumer matters. The list is not exhaustive.

The Criminal Defence Service

Under s 12 of the Access to Justice act 1999, The Legal services Commission established a Legal Defence Service. This service is aimed at ' securing that individuals involved in criminal investigations or proceedings have access to such advice, assistance or representation as the interests of justice require'. The following schemes are offered:

Duty Solicitors

Section 13 of the Access to Justice Act 1999 states that the Commission shall fund advice and assistance as it considers appropriate for individuals who are arrested and held in custody. However, solicitors can no longer attend at a police station, unless the client is vulnerable, where the client is detained for:

• a non-imprisonable offence
• on a warrant
• in breach of bail conditions
• for drink drive offences.

Advice and assistance

This is limited to several hours work and can only include advocacy if the solicitor has applied for a representation order which has been refused. Usually, there is a means test for advice and assistance. However, a duty solicitor at a magistrates court can see all defendants in custody free of charge under the advice and assistance scheme.

Representation

This covers the costs of a solicitor to prepare the defence before the case gets to court. It also covers representation at court, including issues such as bail. If a barrister is required then this will be covered. There will be a merits case for representation and the judge can also order the defendant to pay some of the costs at the end of the trial.

Glossary of terms

Advocacy-Arguments usually addressed to a court

Attorney General-A law officer of the Crown who represents and advises the Government on legal issues. Is responsible for presenting report on the operation of the CPS to Parliament.

Bail-The process by which the court or the police decide whether a suspect/defendant should be released into the community until a trial date or further questioning.

Bench-Where more than one lay magistrate sit together to hear a case they are referred to as the bench.

Chief Crown Prosecutor-Member of the Crown prosecution Service who has the responsibility for the day-to-day operations of a Crown Prosecution area.

Clerk to the Justice-Responsible for the administration within the magistrate's court. Provides advice on legal procedures, such as sentencing issues, to magistrates.

Codes of Practice-Written documents created by the Home Secretary under the Police and Criminal Evidence Act 1984, which provide information and guidance for police regarding use of their powers.

Common law-Judge-made law, developed on a case-by-case basis. Also referred to as case law, developed through the doctrine of judicial precedent.

Conditional bail-form of bail with conditions attached, such as agreeing to keep away from certain places etc.

County court-First instance court that deals with low value, non-complex cases.

Cross-examination-The process by which a lawyer can question an opposing party's witnesses or even the defendant in order to enhance their clients case.

Crown court-Criminal first instance court, hears indictable offences/triable either way offences-jury determines guilt or innocence of the accused-judge administers sentence.

Crown Prosecution Service-The primary agency responsible for prosecuting individuals who have committed criminal offences within England and Wales. Also determines the charge that will be laid before individuals based on police evidence.

Custodial sentence-A form of sentence administered by the courts. Most severe form of punishment-defendant is detained, for instance, in prison to serve a sentence determined by the court.

Director of Public Prosecutions-Head of the Crown Prosecution Service. Can undertake criminal prosecutions in his or her own right.

District Judge (magistrates court)-Legally qualified magistrate who can sit and hear case on own-presides over cases in the magistrate's court.

Equity-A form of law based on principles of natural justice and fairness.

European Court of Human Rights-Court that hears infringements of the European Convention on Rights and Fundamental Freedoms.

European Court of Justice-Court of the European Union which is responsible for hearing actions between Member State, between Institutions and the Member States and between EU Institutions themselves. Also responsible for ensuring uniform interpretation and application of European Union law throughout the Member States.

Hearing-The oral submission in the litigation before the court, tribunal etc.

High Court-First instance civil court hears complex and high value cases. Three divisions: Family, Queens Bench and Chancery.

Hybrid offences-also known as triable either way offences. Offences of varying degrees of seriousness which may be heard by the crown.

Inadmissable evidence-Evidence which is not admitted into the trial proper. This may be that the evidence has been obtained in an improper manner.

Indictable offences-Most serious form of criminal offences, such as murder, rape, which can only be dealt with by the Crown Court.

Judicial precedent-The foundation of the development t of modern common law/case law. Process by which members of the judiciary follow previous case decisions where facts are similar.

Judicial review-A higher court's supervision of a tribunal's procedure.

Lay magistrate-A layperson, ordinary member of the public without legal experience who can sit within magistrate's courts determining guilt or innocence of defendants, sentencing issues, etc.
Layperson-A member of the public without legal experience who plays a role in the English legal system.

Legal Executives-Members of the Institute of Legal Executives who may have rights of audience in some courts.

Legal Services Commission-Government Agency responsible for administering legal aid, legal representation etc.

Magistrates court-First instance court which has primarily criminal jurisdiction but also some civil jurisdiction.

Majority verdict-Verdict where those in favour of a particular verdict outweigh those opposing.

Mitigating circumstances-Circumstances particular to a defendant, which are taken into account by the courts when determining sentence.

Obiter dicta-Latin phrase which literally means 'things said by the way'.

Original precedent-The first decision on a particular legal problem which is novel in nature.

Practice directions-Instructions issued by a court concerning the conduct of cases generally.

Pre-action protocols-Standard steps which each party should effect prior to issuing a claim or prior to a hearing.

Proceedings-Steps to start or pursue a case in court.

Ratio-decidendi Latin phrase, literally meaning, reason for the decision'. The binding element of a judgement.

Remand-Where a person has been refused bail, he or she will be held in custody until the trial takes place.

Representation-Appearing on behalf of a client.

Rights of audience-The right to appear as a lawyer in a particular court.

Royal assent-Monarch gives formal approval to a bill becoming an Act of Parliament.

Sentence-Pronouncement of the court, which highlights a form of punishment that is to be imposed on a defendant convicted of a criminal offence.

Summary offences-Minor criminal offences that can only be heard in the magistrates court.

Triable either way offences-Offences of varying degrees of seriousness which may be heard in the Crown Court or magistrates court.

Tribunal-A panel authorized to adjudicate on specific matters.

Ultra vires-Acting beyond powers given.

Youth Court-A special court within the magistrate's court which hears criminal cases involving young offenders.

English Legal System Websites

Administrative Justice & Tribunals Council http://ajtc.justice.gov.uk/

Attorney General http://www.attorneygeneral.gov.uk/

Bar Council www.barcouncil.org.uk

British and Irish Legal information Institute http://www.bailii.org/

Centre for Effective Dispute Resolution (ADR)
http://www.cedr.co.uk/

Criminal Cases Review Commission
http://www.justice.gov.uk/about/criminal-cases-review-commission

Criminal Courts Review 2002, national archives
http://webarchive.nationalarchives.gov.uk/+/http://criminal-courts-review.org.uk/

Crown Prosecution Service www.cps.gov.uk

Department of Constitutional Affairs (predecessor, Ministry of Justice), national archives
http://webarchive.nationalarchives.gov.uk/*/http://www.dca.gov.uk/

European Court of Human Rights http://www.echr.coe.int/echr

EC and EU institution and EC documents, including European Commission and European Court of Justice http://europa.eu/

European Commission Representation in the UK, for EU news, publications, info and free email newsletter
http://ec.europa.eu/unitedkingdom/

UK Government information
http://www.direct.gov.uk/Homepage/fs/en

Her Majesty's Courts & Tribunals Service
http://www.justice.gov.uk/about/hmcts/

Home Office www.homeoffice.gov.uk

International Courts of Justice are best accessed via the UN website
http://www.un.org/

Judiciary http://www.judiciary.gov.uk/

Judicial Appointments Commission http://jac.judiciary.gov.uk/

Judicial College http://www.judiciary.gov.uk/training-support/judicial-college

Judicial Committee of the Privy Council http://www.jcpc.gov.uk/

Law Commission http://lawcommission.justice.gov.uk/
Law Society http://www.lawsociety.org.uk
Law Society's Gazette: http://www.lawgazette.co.uk/home.law
Legal Abbreviations, contains 12,500 abbreviations
http://www.legalabbrevs.cardiff.ac.uk/
Legal Action Group www.lag.org.uk
Legal Services Commission www.legalservices.gov.uk
Legislation http://legislation.gov.uk/
Lexis is a very comprehensive database. Access it via your library's e-resources.
Liberty www.liberty-human-rights.org.uk
Ministry of Justice http://www.justice.gov.uk/
National Assembly for Wales http://www.assemblywales.org/index.htm
Parliament www.parliament.uk
Scottish Parliament: www.scottish.parliament.uk
The Times http://www.timesonline.co.uk
UK Newsstand, all UK newspapers is available via your library's e-resources.
UK Supreme Court http://supremecourt.gov.uk/index.html
US Supreme Court www.supremecourtus.gov
Westlaw, another very comprehensive subscriber database, containing all case law, statute law many law journals and accessed via library e-resources.

Index

Emerald Publishing
www.emeraldpublishing.co.uk

Titles in the Emerald Series:

Law

Guide to Bankruptcy
Conducting Your Own Court case
Guide to Consumer law
Creating a Will
Guide to Family Law
Guide to Employment Law
Guide to European Union Law
Guide to Health and Safety Law
Guide to Criminal Law
Guide to Landlord and Tenant Law
Guide to the English Legal System
Guide to Housing Law
Guide to Marriage and Divorce
Guide to The Civil Partnerships Act
Guide to The Law of Contract
The Path to Justice
You and Your Legal Rights
Powers of Attorney
Managing Divorce

Health

Guide to Combating Child Obesity
Asthma Begins at Home
Alternative Health and Alternative Remedies

Music

How to Survive and Succeed in the Music Industry

General

A Practical Guide to Obtaining probate
A Practical Guide to Residential Conveyancing
Writing The Perfect CV
Keeping Books and Accounts-A Small Business Guide
Business Start Up-A Guide for New Business
Finding Asperger Syndrome in the Family-A Book of Answers
Explaining Autism Spectrum Disorder
Explaining Alzheimers
Explaining Parkinsons
Writing True Crime
Becoming a Professional Writer
Writing your Autobiography

For details of the above titles published by Emerald go to:

www.emeraldpublishing.co.uk